the cocktail bible

hamlyn

the cocktail bible

over 600 cocktails shaken,
stirred and on the rocks

Notes

The measure than has been used in the recipes is based on a bar jigger, which is 25 ml (1 fl oz). If preferred, a different volume can be used providing the proportions are kept constant within a drink and suitable adjustments are made to spoon measurements, where they occur.

Standard level spoon measurements are used throughout.
1 tablespoon = one 15 ml spoon
1 teaspoon = one 5 ml spoon
All recipes serve one unless otherwise specified.

Safety note

The Department of Health advises that eggs should not be consumed raw. This book contains recipes made with raw eggs. It is prudent for more vulnerable people such as pregnant and nursing mothers, invalids and the elderly to avoid these recipes.

First published in Great Britain in 2005 by Hamlyn,
a division of Octopus Publishing Group Ltd
2–4 Heron Quays London E14 4JP

ISBN-13: 978-0-600-61347-3
ISBN-10: 0-600-61347-X

A CIP catalogue record for this book is available from the British Library

Printed and bound in China

10 9 8 7 6 5 4 3 2

Different Types of Cocktail

Short Drinks

These beverages generally consist of one or two main spirits stirred or mixed together, or may sometimes be composed of a spirit and a main mixer. Short drinks are generally served with plenty of ice and have a more concentrated alcohol level or a more even ratio between the alcohol and the amount of mixer, where a mixer is included. An example of a short drink is the French Connection – Cognac and Amaretto are poured into an old-fashioned glass and served over ice. Short drinks are for sipping, so the large quantity of ice ensures that they remain chilled.

Long Drinks

Long drinks may combine a couple of spirits or a mixture of alcohols, served with a larger amount of mixer. There is generally a lower alcohol-to-mixer ratio than in short drinks. An example of this is a Woo Woo: vodka shaken together with peach liqueur, poured into a highball glass and topped up with cranberry juice. Many long drinks have a fruit mixer or they may be topped up with tonic or soda water or cola. Long drinks will often be drunk with a straw and may be decorated with pieces of fruit.

Shots

A shot is basically a small drink served in a specific shot glass, which is designed to be drunk in one short hit. It is usually a combination of a spirit and one or more other flavoured alcohols. However, the most famous shot in its original, purest form – the Tequila Slammer – is just tequila. Salt is licked from the hand first, then the shot is drunk and finally a wedge of lime is sucked to quell the strong flavour of the drink. The ingredients for a shot are often shaken before serving, as with many other cocktails, but the more impressive drinks are skillfully layered into the glass, creating a colourful striped effect that no doubt compensates for the size of the drink and the speed at which it is drunk. Some well-known layered shots include the B-52 (see page 225), which combines Baileys with Grand Marnier and Kahlúa. The art of the layered shot comes down to an understanding of physics, as heavier alcohols must be added to the glass first, with lighter ones coming after, so that the layers stay in the order in which they have been added to the glass.

the ingredients. Once ready, the drink is poured from one of the containers. The European Shaker is the more classic style that we are used to seeing in stores and one that is probably safer for a novice mixologist. It's generally made from metal and is just one conical-shaped container over which a tight-fitting top is placed. This will generally have holes in the middle that act as the strainer, and a cap fits snugly over this.

Free-pouring is fine when you are serving spirits with mixers, but when it comes to making cocktails, a little more precision is required, so a set of measures is another essential item for your bar. Many cocktails have exact measurements of alcohol and any deviation will alter the final flavour, so it's important to follow the recipe exactly. Measures (or jiggers as they are sometimes called) can vary in their exact volume, so check the quantity of one measure before you start mixing, in order to prevent your guests from inebriation after their first drink.

Another absolute essential for cocktail-making is ice. You really can't have enough of it, so make sure you prepare plenty in advance or, better still, buy a couple of large bags of ice to keep in the freezer. Ice is used in most cocktails as a means

Different Types of Cocktail

Short Drinks

These beverages generally consist of one or two main spirits stirred or mixed together, or may sometimes be composed of a spirit and a main mixer. Short drinks are generally served with plenty of ice and have a more concentrated alcohol level or a more even ratio between the alcohol and the amount of mixer, where a mixer is included. An example of a short drink is the French Connection – Cognac and Amaretto are poured into an old-fashioned glass and served over ice. Short drinks are for sipping, so the large quantity of ice ensures that they remain chilled.

Long Drinks

Long drinks may combine a couple of spirits or a mixture of alcohols, served with a larger amount of mixer. There is generally a lower alcohol-to-mixer ratio than in short drinks. An example of this is a Woo Woo: vodka shaken together with peach liqueur, poured into a highball glass and topped up with cranberry juice. Many long drinks have a fruit mixer or they may be topped up with tonic or soda water or cola. Long drinks will often be drunk with a straw and may be decorated with pieces of fruit.

Shots

A shot is basically a small drink served in a specific shot glass, which is designed to be drunk in one short hit. It is usually a combination of a spirit and one or more other flavoured alcohols. However, the most famous shot in its original, purest form – the Tequila Slammer – is just tequila. Salt is licked from the hand first, then the shot is drunk and finally a wedge of lime is sucked to quell the strong flavour of the drink. The ingredients for a shot are often shaken before serving, as with many other cocktails, but the more impressive drinks are skillfully layered into the glass, creating a colourful striped effect that no doubt compensates for the size of the drink and the speed at which it is drunk. Some well-known layered shots include the B-52 (see page 225), which combines Baileys with Grand Marnier and Kahlúa. The art of the layered shot comes down to an understanding of physics, as heavier alcohols must be added to the glass first, with lighter ones coming after, so that the layers stay in the order in which they have been added to the glass.

Bar Basics

In order to be able to offer your guests a selection of drinks, or indeed to have a choice of drinks for yourself at home, there are certain ingredients that should always be present in your bar. These include a range of basic spirits, mixers, flavourings and other alcoholic drinks that are commonly used in cocktails. To start with the spirits, you should stock your bar with the following essentials: vodka, gin, tequila, whisky, brandy and rum. Champagne and wine are necessary for certain cocktails, but this depends on whether you plan to serve a select few cocktails of your choosing, or whether guests can select their own drinks themselves. If you're going to make shots, you will need to extend your bar to include other drinks such as Baileys, Crème de menthe, Kahlúa, Amaretto and Crème de cacao. There are literally hundreds of flavoured liqueurs and spirits, so, if you are preparing shots, it's probably best to first identify a couple of favourites and then buy the ingredients for those, otherwise you could end up with a whole cupboard full of only partly used bottles of expensive alcohol that will never be touched again.

When it comes to mixers, you can't go too far wrong with staples such as tonic and soda water, a selection of fruit juices, lemonade and cola. Other ingredients that will come in handy include seasonings such as salt, pepper, Tabasco sauce and Worcestershire sauce, as well as a selection of different fruit for decorations, cocktail cherries, olives, mint leaves and, of course, plenty of lemons and limes, both for decoration as well as for the juice itself.

Glasses and Equipment

Although cocktails can be created with a minimum of good-quality ingredients and a flair for mixing, certain pieces of equipment are absolutely essential for even the most basic bar. You don't need to spend a lot of money and you may find that you already own some of the equipment and glasses you'll need for a successful cocktail party. The key is to have everything ready well in advance, just in case you need to do any last-minute shopping.

Glasses

There is really no point even considering a cocktail evening if you don't have a basic selection of glasses. While cheap wine glasses and plastic cups are perfectly acceptable for a barbecue, they just won't do for cocktails. Part of the appeal of the cocktail is the aesthetics, and while you may spend ages lovingly preparing and mixing a drink, following the recipe to the letter and adding a beautifully crafted decoration, if you serve it in an inappropriate glass or a cheap plastic cup, all your hard work will be wasted. Cocktails should look good as well as taste great, and you'll be fighting a losing battle if you dust off those glasses you got free at the local garage for the job.

At the very least you will need the following glasses to cover the basic drinks that you might want to prepare. An old-fashioned (or rocks or lowball) glass or tumbler will be required for simple mixed spirits or short drinks – this glass is usually wide and low with a heavy base.

A highball glass is slimmer and taller and this is used for long drinks. Champagne flutes are a must if you're planning on serving any Champagne or sparkling wine cocktails. These are delicate glasses with long stems and a slim body that helps to keep the bubbles intact. A Martini glass is the classic cocktail glass and can be used to serve any number of drinks, including the Martini. They have sloping sides that form a 'V' shape and a long stem. They are designed this way so that there is minimum contact between your hand and the actual glass, to avoid warming the drink. If you're planning a party, you should really invest in a set of these. Last but not least, a set of shot glasses will be required if you plan on serving shots. Although you may try and get away with accurate measuring, it could all get very messy if you start serving shot drinks from old-fashioned glasses. It's a good idea to have more glasses than you think you'll need, as inevitably a couple will break or get left on a bookshelf or tucked under a table and forgotten.

Essential Equipment

Apart from glasses, your main piece of equipment is the shaker. There are two basic types: the Boston Shaker and the European Cocktail Shaker. The Boston Shaker is literally two containers that are slightly conical in shape and one of which is often made from glass. The ingredients are added to one, then they are both pushed together to form a sealed unit and this is shaken to combine

the ingredients. Once ready, the drink is poured from one of the containers. The European Shaker is the more classic style that we are used to seeing in stores and one that is probably safer for a novice mixologist. It's generally made from metal and is just one conical-shaped container over which a tight-fitting top is placed. This will generally have holes in the middle that act as the strainer, and a cap fits snugly over this.

Free-pouring is fine when you are serving spirits with mixers, but when it comes to making cocktails, a little more precision is required, so a set of measures is another essential item for your bar. Many cocktails have exact measurements of alcohol and any deviation will alter the final flavour, so it's important to follow the recipe exactly. Measures (or jiggers as they are sometimes called) can vary in their exact volume, so check the quantity of one measure before you start mixing, in order to prevent your guests from inebriation after their first drink.

Another absolute essential for cocktail-making is ice. You really can't have enough of it, so make sure you prepare plenty in advance or, better still, buy a couple of large bags of ice to keep in the freezer. Ice is used in most cocktails as a means

of chilling the ingredients while they're being shaken or stirred, and it is also used to chill the actual glasses while the drink is being prepared. An ice bucket and tongs are good to have, but there's no need to buy them especially for the occasion – a wine cooler or large plastic container and a serving spoon should do the trick. Crushed ice is required in a number of drinks and, although you can buy a little gadget that will do all the hard work for you, a clean tea towel and a rolling pin will have a similar effect.

Most kitchens are equipped with a selection of sharp knives, but if for some reason yours isn't, this is something you'll need to buy. A small, sharp knife is necessary for cutting citrus slices and wedges, as well as chopping herbs and other

garnishes. The same goes for a chopping board, which you'll probably also already have.

Optional Extras

There is an endless list of little gizmos and accessories that you can buy for the preparation of cocktails, but unless you plan on hosting serious cocktail parties on a regular basis, then you can probably manage with just the essentials listed above. Having said that, cocktail equipment always makes interesting birthday present ideas or stocking fillers and there are some really quirky little gadgets around that any drinks aficionado would be more than happy to receive. If you're using a Boston Shaker to prepare your drinks, then a strainer is a useful tool to have on hand. Guests don't want big chunks of ice or fruit seeds floating around

in their drink, so you use this when pouring the liquid into the serving glass. It usually has a metal lip, which sits neatly on the side of the shaker to stop it slipping as the final drops pour through. While a regular spoon will probably be sufficient, a specific spoon called a bar spoon will do the job a lot more effectively. It's basically a small spoon on a very long handle, which is used to stir long drinks, getting right down to the bottom of the glass. The handle of the spoon is often twisted as well, which means it can be used to add small amounts of ingredients to drinks that need to sit on top or are delicate. The liquid is poured from the bottle on to the top of the spoon and then gradually and evenly makes its way down and around the handle until it reaches the surface of the drink itself.

Cocktail sticks will add a little something extra to your cocktails. Available in materials ranging from the basic wood to brightly coloured plastic in varying shapes, you'll need these if you're serving drinks with decorations such as olives or fruit. Cocktail paper parasols are considered by some to be essential for adding a fun finishing touch to your drink. Likewise, straws can add a fun decorative element to your drinks and are available in all manner of different colours and styles.

Tips and Techniques

You don't need any special skills to make cocktails and to begin with there are really just two simple rules to remember: make sure you have all the correct ingredients to hand before you start, and secondly, follow the recipe carefully. You shouldn't go too far wrong with most basic drinks, and once you begin to get a little more confident, you can try experimenting with more complicated recipes involving layering or setting drinks alight! If you do want to hone your skills as a cocktail mixologist, there are numerous techniques that can be practised to give your mixing skills a bit of flair and make the whole experience more enjoyable for you and your guests. One easy tip is to put serving glasses in the freezer an hour or so before you start preparing drinks. You'll often see this done in bars, not just for cocktails but for lager as well, and it really will make a difference to the finished drink if the glass is icy cold.

Shaking

A good technique to perfect early on in your cocktail career is shaking. Not only will your energetic display impress your guests, but it is essential for authentic-tasting cocktails. Whether you're using a Boston or European shaker, it's important to shake that drink like your life depends on it – the ingredients will combine thoroughly and the ice will circulate well, ensuring that the drink is well chilled when you come to pour it.

Stirring

If a drink requires stirring, then stir as gently as you can using a bar spoon – you don't want the ice to crack and break, as this will only water down and subsequently dilute the drink. You also don't want too much air incorporated into the drink by stirring too vigorously.

Layering

Discussed earlier, this is a technique often used to make shots. Use the back of a bar spoon to gently pour each ingredient into the glass, one after the other, without it breaking the surface of the ingredient below. There should be a very definite layer to each ingredient.

Muddling

Some recipes will ask you to 'muddle' ingredients. This means using a bar spoon to mulch down the flavouring ingredients in the glass before adding the alcohol. So, for example, in the Caipirinha (see page 219), cane sugar and lime quarters are muddled together before the Cachaça is added.

Decorating Cocktails

Some cocktails are decorated for decoration's sake, while for others the decoration is a vital part of the flavour (the olive in a Martini is one example of this). Decoration can range from a simple twist of lime to a complicated assemblage of fruit pieces on a cocktail stick, but all add something extra to the finished drink.

Frosting

This is where the rim of the glass is dipped first in water or egg white, or moistened with the juice of a lemon or lime, and then into a flavouring, to decorate it. The most famous example is the Margarita (see page 183), which is dipped in salt, but for other drinks the rim might be dipped in sugar, cocoa powder or cinnamon – it all depends on the ingredients of the drink.

Fruit Wedges

Lemon and lime are the most popular decorations and are used in a number of drinks. They can either be simply dropped into the finished drink, or you can squeeze a little juice into the glass and then drop the wedge into the drink. Alternatively, for a real citrus zing, wipe the wedge around the rim of the glass first. Other fruit, such as pineapples or mangos, can be cut into small wedge shapes, cut halfway through with a sharp knife and positioned over the edge of the glass.

Citrus Rind Spirals

These can be made from lemons, limes or oranges and add a dash of colour to a cocktail. You need to carefully peel a long piece of rind from the fruit, using a parer or a small, sharp knife. Once you have a suitable length, wrap it around a straw and hold it for a few minutes. As the moisture begins to dry, the rind will keep its twisty shape and you can balance it over the edge of a glass. It's a good idea to try and make a few of these citrus spirals in advance.

Citrus Rind Twists

Similar to a spiral, but you start by cutting a wider piece of citrus rind. You can use a vegetable peeler for this and again, balance on the side of the glass or rest briefly over the drink and squeeze to release the oil, before dropping the twist in the drink. You could also try tying them in bows or knots and then arranging them over the drink.

Cherries and Olives

These are generally threaded onto cocktail sticks and balanced over the side of the glass but if you're feeling creative, you can try making your own mini fruit kebabs to decorate your drinks – again, try preparing them in advance to save time. Virtually any type of fruit is attractive.

Whisky

There is fierce debate over whether whisky first originated in Ireland or in Scotland, but whichever it was, there is no denying its huge popularity around the world now. Also known as 'the water of life', whisky is made by distilling malted grain. Historically, it began its long career as a somewhat rough, flavoured liquid that was meant to be taken as a medicinal drink to cure anything from dropsy to tiredness. Many refinements in both taste and production techniques have resulted in the rather more smooth spirit that we are familiar with today. Whisky is sold either as a single unblended spirit or as a blended whisky, which may contain a number of different whiskies that are carefully combined to produce a smooth, flavourful result. Many whisky cocktails have names that refer to the Celtic roots of the spirit, such as Rob Roy, Bobby Burns and Aberdeen Angus.

Rickey

4–5 ice cubes
1½ measures whisky
1½ measures lime juice
soda water, to top up
lime rind twist, to decorate

Put the ice cubes with the
whisky and the lime juice in
a tall glass. Top up with soda
water and stir. Garnish with
a lime rind twist.

Blinker

cracked ice cubes
½ measure Canadian
    whisky
¾ measure grapefruit juice
¼ measure grenadine

Put some cracked ice with the
whisky, grapefruit juice and
grenadine into a cocktail shaker
and shake well. Serve in a
chilled cocktail glass.

Rollin' Stoned

4–5 ice cubes, plus extra
    to serve
2 measures Thai whisky
1 dash banana liqueur
1 dash raspberry liqueur
1 dash lime juice
2 measures orange juice
2 measures pineapple juice
oranges slices, to decorate
cocktail cherries, to
    decorate

Put all the ingredients into a
cocktail shaker. Shake and
strain into a highball glass filled
with ice cubes. Decorate with
orange slices and cherries and
serve with long straws.

Canadian Daisy

4–5 ice cubes, plus extra
   to serve
2 measures Canadian
   whisky
2 teaspoons lemon juice
1 teaspoon raspberry juice
1 teaspoon sugar syrup
soda water, to top up
whole raspberries,
   to decorate
1 teaspoon brandy

Put the ice cubes with the
whisky, fruit juices and sugar
syrup into a cocktail shaker and
shake well. Strain into a tall
glass. Add ice and top up with
soda water. Decorate with
raspberries and float the
brandy on top of the drink.

Early Night

1 tablespoon fresh
   lemon juice
1 measure clear honey
1 measure whisky
2 measures boiling water
1 measure ginger wine
lemon slice, to decorate

Put the lemon juice and honey
into a toddy glass and stir well.
Add the whisky and continue
stirring. Stir in the boiling
water, then add the ginger wine.
Decorate with a lemon slice.
Stir continuously while
drinking it hot.

Nerida

4–5 ice cubes
juice of ½ lime or lemon
3 measures Scotch whisky
dry ginger ale, to top up
lime or lemon slices,
   to decorate

Put the ice cubes, lime or lemon
juice and whisky into a cocktail
shaker and shake until a frost
forms. Pour without straining
into a chilled Collins glass. Top
up with dry ginger ale and stir
gently. Decorate with lime or
lemon slices.

Mississippi Punch

crushed ice
3 drops Angostura bitters
1 teaspoon sugar syrup
juice of 1 lemon
1 measure brandy
1 measure dark rum
2 measures bourbon
    whiskey

Half-fill a tall glass with
crushed ice. Shake the bitters
over the ice. Pour in the sugar
syrup and the lemon juice, then
stir gently to mix thoroughly.
Add the brandy, rum and
bourbon, in that order, stir
once and serve with straws.

Benedict

3–4 ice cubes
1 measure Bénédictine
3 measures whisky
dry ginger ale, to top up

Put the ice cubes into a mixing
glass. Pour the Bénédictine
and whisky over the ice. Stir
evenly without splashing. Pour
without straining into a chilled
highball glass. Top up with dry
ginger ale.

Leprechaun Dancer

4–5 ice cubes
1 measure Irish whiskey
1 measure lemon juice
soda water, to top up
dry ginger ale, to top up
lemon rind twist, to
    decorate

Combine the ice cubes, whiskey
and lemon juice in a highball
glass. Top up with soda water
and dry ginger ale in equal
measures. Decorate with a
lemon rind twist.

Big Butt

1 strawberry, hulled
3 raspberries
3 blueberries, plus extra
   to decorate
2 teaspoons Chambord
1 dash fresh lime juice
2 measures Buffalo Trace
   bourbon whiskey
3 measures cranberry juice
4–5 ice cubes

Muddle the berries and
Chambord in a cocktail shaker.
Add the lime juice, bourbon,
cranberry juice and ice cubes.
Shake, then pour without
straining into a highball glass
and decorate with blueberries.

Did you know?
Buffalo Trace bourbon has a
delicious vanilla character that
complements fruity drinks.

Rhett Butler

4–5 ice cubes, plus extra
   to serve
2 measures bourbon
   whiskey
4 measures cranberry juice
2 tablespoons sugar syrup
1 tablespoon fresh lime
   juice
lime slices, to decorate

Put the ice cubes with the
bourbon, cranberry juice, sugar
syrup and lime juice into a
cocktail shaker and shake well.
Fill an old-fashioned glass with
ice cubes and strain the cocktail
over them. Decorate with lime
slices and serve with straws.

Capricorn

4–5 ice cubes, cracked
1 measure bourbon whiskey
½ measure apricot brandy
½ measure lemon juice
2 measures orange juice
orange slice, to decorate

Put half the cracked ice cubes
into a cocktail shaker and add
the whiskey, apricot brandy
and the lemon and orange
juices. Shake to mix. Put the
remaining ice into an old-
fashioned glass and strain the
cocktail over them. Decorate
with an orange slice.

Mint Julep I

10 mint leaves
1 teaspoon sugar syrup
4 dashes Angostura bitters
crushed ice
2 measures bourbon
    whiskey
mint sprig, to decorate

Muddle the mint leaves, sugar syrup and bitters in a highball glass. Fill the glass with crushed ice. then add the bourbon. Stir well and decorate with a mint sprig.

Did you know?
The earliest written reference to that ultimate Deep South cocktail, the Mint Julep, dates to 1803.

Mint Julep II

3 sprigs mint, plus extra
    to decorate
½ tablespoon caster sugar
1 tablespoon soda water
2–3 ice cubes
1 measure bourbon whiskey

Crush the mint with the caster sugar in an old-fashioned glass or large tumbler and rub it around the insides of the glass. Discard the mint. Dissolve the sugar in the soda water, add the ice and pour over the Bourbon. Do not stir. Decorate with the extra sprig of mint.

Virginia Mint Julep

9 young mint sprigs, plus
    extra to decorate
1 teaspoon sugar syrup
crushed ice
3 measures bourbon
    whiskey

Muddle the mint and sugar syrup in an iced silver mug or tall glass. Fill the mug or glass with crushed ice, pour the bourbon over the ice and stir gently. Pack in more crushed ice and stir until a frost forms. Wrap the mug or glass in a table napkin and serve decorated with a mint sprig.

A Kiwi in Tennessee

½ kiwi fruit, peeled
2 measures Jack Daniel's
1 measure kiwi fruit
　　schnapps
1 measure fresh lemon juice
ice cubes
lemonade, to top up
kiwi fruit slices, to decorate

Muddle the kiwi fruit in a cocktail shaker, then add the whiskey, schnapps and lemon juice. Add some ice cubes and shake well. Strain into a highball glass filled with ice cubes. Stir and top up with lemonade. Decorate with kiwi fruit slices.

Lynchburg Lemonade

ice cubes
1½ measures Jack Daniel's
1 measure Cointreau
1 measure fresh lemon juice
lemonade, to top up
lemon slices, to decorate

Put some ice cubes with the whiskey, Cointreau and lemon juice into a cocktail shaker and shake well. Strain into a highball glass filled with ice cubes. Top up with lemonade and stir. Decorate with lemon slices.

Did you know?
A classic based on Jack Daniel's 'sour mash' Tennessee whiskey, this cocktail was specially created for the Jack Daniel's distillery in Lynchburg, Tennessee.

Eclipse

4–5 ice cubes
2 measures Jack Daniel's
½ measure Chambord
½ measure lime juice
1 dash sugar syrup
1 measure cranberry juice
1 measure raspberry juice
raspberry and lime wedge,
　　to decorate

Put the ice cubes with the other ingredients into a cocktail shaker and shake well. Strain into a large highball glass filled with crushed ice. Serve with long straws and decorate with a raspberry and a lime wedge.

Irish Coffee

1 measure Irish whiskey
hot filter coffee
lightly whipped cream
ground coffee, to decorate

Put a bar spoon into a large
wine glass, add the whiskey,
then top up with hot coffee
and stir. Heat the cream very
slightly and pour into the
bowl of the spoon on top of
the coffee to get a good float.
Decorate with a pinch of
ground coffee.

Kicker

1 measure whisky
1 measure Midori
ice cubes, to serve
    (optional)

Combine the whisky and
Midori in a mixing glass and
serve chilled or on the rocks.

Tar

4–5 ice cubes
juice of 1 lemon
½ teaspoon grenadine
1 measure crème de cacao
3 measures whisky

Put the ice cubes into a cocktail
shaker. Pour in the lemon
juice, grenadine, crème de
cacao and whisky and shake
until a frost forms. Strain into
a chilled cocktail glass. Serve
with a straw.

Rattlesnake

4–5 ice cubes, plus extra
   to serve
1½ measures whisky
1 teaspoon lemon juice
1 teaspoon sugar syrup
1 egg white
few drops Pernod

Put all the ingredients into
a cocktail shaker and shake
extremely well. Strain into a
glass and add more ice.

Southerly
Buster

4–5 ice cubes
1 measure blue Curaçao
3 measures whisky
lemon rind strip, to decorate

Put the ice cubes into a mixing
glass. Pour the Curaçao and
whisky over the ice, stir
vigorously, then strain into a
chilled cocktail glass. Twist
the lemon rind strip over the
drink and drop it in. Serve
with a straw.

Harlequin

5 white grapes, plus
   2 to decorate
½ measure sweet vermouth
6 dashes orange bitters
crushed ice
2 measures Canadian
   Club whisky

Muddle the white grapes,
vermouth and bitters in an
old-fashioned glass. Half-fill
the glass with crushed ice and
stir well. Add the whisky and
top up with crushed ice.
Decorate with the extra grapes.

Did you know?
Canadian Club whisky is aged
in white oak, giving it a lighter,
smoother taste than most Scotches
and bourbons. It works particularly
well with sweet vermouth in this
elegant cocktail.

Roamin' the Gloamin'

4–5 ice cubes
2 measures Scotch whisky
1 measure Cointreau
2 tablespoons fresh
    orange juice
orange slice, to decorate

Put the ice cubes into a cocktail
shaker. Add the whisky,
Cointreau and orange juice and
shake until a frost forms. Pour
into an old-fashioned glass and
decorate with an orange slice.

Whisky Mac

3–4 ice cubes
1 measure Scotch whisky
1 measure ginger wine

Put the ice cubes into an
old-fashioned glass. Pour the
whisky and ginger wine over
the ice and stir slightly.

Bobby Burns

4–5 cubes
1 measure Scotch whisky
1 measure dry vermouth
1 tablespoon Bénédictine
lemon rind strip, to decorate

Put the ice cubes with the
whisky, vermouth and
Bénédictine into a cocktail
shaker and shake until a frost
forms. Strain into a chilled
cocktail glass and decorate
with a lemon rind strip.

Club

3 ice cubes, cracked
2 dashes Angostura bitters
1 measure Scotch whisky
1 dash grenadine
lemon rind spiral, to
    decorate
cocktail cherry, to decorate

Put the ice into a mixing glass.
Add the bitters, whisky and
grenadine and stir well. Strain
into a cocktail glass and
decorate with a lemon rind
spiral and a cherry.

Rob Roy

1 ice cube, cracked
1 measure Scotch whisky
½ measure vermouth
1 dash Angostura bitters
lemon rind spiral, to
    decorate

Put the cracked ice, whisky,
vermouth and bitters into a
mixing glass and stir well.
Strain into a cocktail glass and
decorate the rim with a lemon
rind spiral.

Rusty Nail

ice cubes
1½ measures Scotch whisky
1 measure Drambuie

Fill an old-fashioned glass with
ice cubes and pour over the
Scotch whisky and Drambuie.
Stir gently.

Did you know?

Rob Roy was an historical character
and the eponymous hero of a novel
by Sir Walter Scott. A powerful,
dangerous outlaw and Jacobite
sympathizer, he was also renowned
for his kindness and generosity to
the oppressed – a kind of Scottish
Robin Hood, much admired in
Scottish folk history.

New Yorker

2–3 ice cubes, cracked
1 measure Scotch whisky
1 teaspoon fresh lime juice
1 teaspoon icing sugar
finely grated rind
    of ½ lemon
lemon rind spiral,
    to decorate

Put the cracked ice into a cocktail shaker and add the whisky, lime juice and sugar. Shake until a frost forms. Strain into a cocktail glass. Sprinkle the grated lemon rind over the surface and decorate the rim with a lemon rind spiral.

Did you know?
Orange bitters are made from alcohol infused with the rind of Seville oranges, and have a concentrated bitter-sweet orange flavour.

Silky Pin

ice cubes
1 measure Scotch whisky
1 measure Drambuie
    Cream Liqueur

Fill an old-fashioned glass with ice cubes and pour over the whisky and Drambuie Cream Liqueur. Stir gently.

Whizz Bang

4–5 ice cubes
3 drops orange bitters
½ teaspoon grenadine
1 measure dry vermouth
3 measures Scotch whisky
1 drop Pernod

Put the ice cubes into a mixing glass. Shake the bitters over the ice and pour in the grenadine, vermouth and whisky. Stir vigorously, then strain into a chilled cocktail glass. Add the Pernod and stir.

Aberdeen Angus

2 measures Scotch whisky
1 measure Drambuie
1 teaspoon clear honey
2 teaspoons lime juice

Combine the whisky and the honey in a mug and stir until smooth. Add the lime juice. Warm the Drambuie in a small saucepan over a low heat. Pour into a ladle, ignite and pour into the mug. Stir and serve immediately.

Zoom

ice cubes
2 measures Scotch whisky
1 teaspoon clear honey
1 measure chilled water
1 measure single cream

Put the ice cubes into a cocktail shaker, add the whisky, honey, chilled water and cream and shake well. Strain into an old-fashioned glass and serve at once.

Italian Heather

4–5 ice cubes
4 measures Scotch whisky
1 measure Galliano
lemon rind twist,
    to decorate

Put the ice cubes into a tall glass and stir in the whisky and Galliano. Decorate with a lemon rind twist.

Whisky Sour

ice cubes
2 measures whisky
1½ measures fresh
   lemon juice
1 egg white
2 tablespoons caster sugar
4 dashes Angostura bitters
lemon slice and cocktail
   cherry, to decorate

Put some ice cubes with the whisky, lemon juice, egg white, sugar and bitters into a shaker and shake well. Strain into a sour glass filled with ice cubes and decorate with a lemon slice and a cherry on a cocktail stick.

Did you know?

An inspired blend of sour, from the lemon juice, and sweet, this is probably the best known and best-loved sour. The egg white thickens the drink and smoothes it, giving it a foamy head and heavy texture.

Ritz Old-fashioned

lightly beaten egg white
caster sugar
3 ice cubes, crushed
1½ measures bourbon
   whiskey
½ measure Grand Marnier
1 dash lemon juice
1 dash Angostura bitters
orange or lemon slice,
   to decorate
cocktail cherry, to decorate

Frost the rim of an old-fashioned glass by dipping into the egg white, then pressing into the sugar. Put the crushed ice into a cocktail shaker and add the bourbon, Grand Marnier, lemon juice and bitters. Shake to mix, then strain into a glass. Decorate with the orange or lemon slice and a cherry.

Bourbon Peach Smash

6 mint leaves
3 peach slices
3 lemon slices
2 teaspoons caster sugar
2 measures bourbon
   whiskey
ice cubes, plus crushed
   ice to serve
mint sprig, to decorate
lemon slice, to decorate

Muddle the mint leaves, peach and lemon slices and sugar in a cocktail shaker. Add the bourbon and some ice cubes and shake well. Strain over crushed ice in an old-fashioned glass. Decorate with a mint sprig and a lemon slice and serve with short straws.

Bourbon Peach Smash ▶

Golden Daisy

4–5 ice cubes
juice of 1 lemon
1 teaspoon sugar syrup
½ measure Cointreau
3 measures whisky
lime wedge, to decorate

Put the ice cubes into a cocktail shaker. Pour the lemon juice, syrup, Cointreau and whisky over the ice and shake until a frost forms. Strain into an old-fashioned glass and decorate with a lime wedge.

Did you know?
Daisies are refreshing, spirit-based drinks, dating from the nineteenth century, that include grenadine or a sweet liqueur and lemon or lime juice. The Whisky Daisy is probably the best known.

Vanilla Daisy

crushed ice
2 measures bourbon whiskey
1 measure fresh lemon juice
1 measure vanilla syrup
1 teaspoon grenadine
2 cocktail cherries, to decorate

Put some crushed ice with the bourbon, lemon juice and vanilla syrup into a cocktail shaker and shake well. Strain into an old-fashioned glass filled with crushed ice, then drizzle the grenadine through the drink. Decorate with cocktail cherries.

Whisky Daisy

ice cubes
2 measures Scotch whisky or bourbon whiskey
1 measure fresh lemon juice
1 teaspoon caster sugar
1 teaspoon grenadine
soda water, to top up
lemon rind spiral, to decorate

Put some ice cubes with the whisky, lemon juice, sugar and grenadine in a cocktail shaker and shake well. Strain into an old-fashioned glass filled with ice cubes and top up with soda water, if you like. Decorate with a lemon rind spiral.

Suburban

4–5 ice cubes
3 drops orange or
    Angostura bitters
3 measures bourbon
    whiskey or Scotch whisky
1 measure port
1 measure dark rum

Put the ice cubes into a mixing
glass. Shake the bitters over
the ice and pour in the whisky,
port and rum. Stir vigorously,
then strain into a chilled
cocktail glass.

Bourbon Fixed

ice cubes
2 measures bourbon
    whiskey
1 measure morello cherry
    purée
1 tablespoon fresh lime
    juice
2 teaspoons sugar syrup
lime rind spirals, to
    decorate

Put some ice cubes with the
bourbon, cherry purée, lime
juice and sugar syrup into a
cocktail shaker and shake to
mix. Strain into an old-
fashioned glass filled with ice
cubes and decorate with lime
rind spirals.

Godfather

ice cubes
2 measures J&B Rare
    Scotch whisky
1 measure Amaretto
    di Saronno

Put some ice cubes with the
whisky and Amaretto into a
cocktail shaker and shake
vigorously. Strain into a small
old-fashioned glass filled with
ice cubes.

Did you know?
A popular variations on this old
classic replaces the Scotch with
vodka to make a Godmother.

Godfather Sour

ice cubes
1½ measures bourbon
    whiskey
1 measure Amaretto di
    Saronno
1 measure lemon juice
1 teaspoon sugar syrup
lemon slices, to decorate

Put some ice cubes with the
whisky, Amaretto, lemon juice
and sugar syrup into a cocktail
shaker and shake well. Strain
into a small old-fashioned glass
filled with ice cubes and
decorate with lemon slices.

St Clement's Manhattan

ice cubes
1 measure orange-infused
    bourbon whiskey
1 measure lemon-infused
    bourbon whiskey
1 tablespoon sweet
    vermouth
4 dashes Angostura bitters
orange and lemon rind
    twists, to decorate

Put the ice cubes with the
whiskies, vermouth and bitters
into a mixing glass and stir
well. Strain into a chilled
cocktail glass and decorate with
orange and lemon rind twists.

Manhattan

4–5 ice cubes
1 measure sweet vermouth
3 measures rye or bourbon
    whiskey
cocktail cherry, to decorate
    (optional)

Put the ice cubes into a mixing
glass. Pour the vermouth and
whiskey over the ice. Stir
vigorously, then strain into a
chilled cocktail glass. Decorate
with a cherry, if you like.

Cassis

4–5 ice cubes
1 measure bourbon whiskey
½ measure dry vermouth
1 teaspoon crème de cassis
2 blueberries, to decorate

Put the ice cubes into a cocktail shaker and pour in the bourbon, vermouth and crème de cassis. Shake well, then strain into a chilled cocktail glass and decorate with blueberries impaled on a cocktail stick.

Algonquin

4–5 ice cubes
1 measure pineapple juice
1 measure dry vermouth
3 measures bourbon
    whiskey or Scotch whisky

Put the ice cubes into a mixing glass. Pour the pineapple juice, vermouth and whisky over the ice. Stir vigorously until nearly frothy, then strain into a chilled cocktail glass. Serve decorated with a cocktail parasol and drink with a straw.

Mike Collins

5–6 ice cubes
juice of 1 lemon
1 tablespoon sugar syrup
3 measures Irish whiskey
orange slice
cocktail cherry
soda water, to top up
orange rind spiral,
    to decorate

Put the ice cubes into a cocktail shaker. Pour the lemon juice, sugar syrup and whiskey over the ice and shake until a frost forms. Pour, without straining, into a tumbler or Collins glass and add the orange slice and cocktail cherry impaled on a cocktail stick. Top up with soda water, stir lightly and serve, decorated with an orange rind spiral.

Did you know?
This is a young member of the famous Collins family of cocktails, of which Tom Collins (see page 84) is the oldest.

Cliquet

4–5 ice cubes
juice of 1 orange
3 measures bourbon
   whiskey or Scotch whisky
1 tablespoon dark rum

Put the ice cubes into a mixing glass. Pour the orange juice, whisky and rum over the ice. Stir vigorously, then strain into a sour glass.

Skipper

4–5 ice cubes
4 drops grenadine
juice of ½ orange
1 measure dry vermouth
3 measures rye whiskey
   or Scotch whisky
orange wedge, to decorate

Put the ice cubes into a mixing glass. Pour the grenadine over the ice and add the orange juice, vermouth and whisky. Stir vigorously until nearly frothy, then pour into a tumbler. Decorate with an orange wedge and serve with a straw.

Barbera

5 ice cubes, cracked
1 measure bourbon whiskey
¾ measure Drambuie
¼ measure Amaretto
   di Saronno
2 dashes orange bitters
lemon rind twist
orange slice, to decorate

Put half the ice with the whiskey, liqueurs and bitters into a mixing glass. Put the remaining ice in a tumbler and strain the cocktail over the ice. Squeeze the zest from the lemon rind over the surface and decorate with an orange slice.

Sicilian Kiss

crushed ice
2 measures Southern
  Comfort
1 measure Amaretto
  di Saronno
lemon slice, to decorate

Put plenty of crushed ice with
the bourbon and Amaretto in
either a squat glass or old-
fashioned glass and stir to mix.
Garnish with a lemon slice.

American Belle

½ measure cherry liqueur
½ measure Amaretto
  di Saronno
½ measure bourbon
  whiskey

Pour the cherry liqueur into a
shot glass. Using the back of
a bar spoon, slowly float the
Amaretto over the cherry
liqueur. Pour the bourbon over
the Ameretto in the same way.

Oriental

4–5 ice cubes
1 measure rye whiskey
½ measure sweet vermouth
½ measure Cointreau
½ measure fresh lime juice

Put the ice cubes into a cocktail
shaker and pour the whiskey,
vermouth, Cointreau and lime
juice over the ice. Shake well
then strain into a chilled
cocktail glass.

Bourbon Sloe Gin

ice cubes, and crushed ice
1½ measures bourbon
    whiskey
½ measure sloe gin
½ measure lemon juice
1 tablespoon sugar syrup
lemon and peach slices,
    to decorate

Put the ice cubes with the bourbon and sloe gin into a cocktail shaker and shake well. Strain into a cocktail glass over crushed ice. Decorate with lemon and peach slices.

Black Jack

¾ measure Jack Daniel's
¾ measure black Sambuca

Pour the Jack Daniel's into a shot glass. Using the back of a bar spoon, slowly float the Sambuca over the Jack Daniel's.

Boomerang

½ measure Jagermeister
½ measure bourbon
    whiskey

Pour the Jagermeister into a shot glass. Using the back of a bar spoon, slowly float the bourbon over the Jagermeister.

Did you know?
Two classic drinks – bourbon whiskey and Jagermeister – are brought together in a Boomerang. They don't like to mix, but they taste great together.

Boomerang ▶

Vodka

Vodka is thought to have originated in either Russia or Poland and it takes its name from 'voda', the Russian word for water. Production can be traced back as far as the ninth century, but the resulting spirit remained a rather rough drink for a long time, and one that was prone to impurities, often flavoured with herbs or spices to disguise the taste. Originally distilled from grain, vodka was eventually made from potatoes, although today most vodkas are once again produced from grain and distilled at high temperatures.

Although vodka isn't left to age like many other spirits, the quality of the ingredients used in its production has a big impact on the final drink. Vodka has become extremely popular in recent years with the introduction of new brands that appeal to a younger audience. You'll find any number of vodka cocktails in bars, from the Harvey Wallbanger to the perennial hair-of-the-dog classic, the Bloody Mary.

Melon Ball

5 ice cubes, cracked
1 measure vodka
1 measure Midori
1 measure orange juice,
    plus extra for topping
    up (optional)
orange slice, to decorate
banana ball, to decorate

Put the cracked ice into a tall
glass or goblet. Pour the vodka,
Midori and orange juice into a
cocktail shaker. Shake well,
then strain into the glass. Top
up with more orange juice, if
necessary. Decorate with an
orange slice and a banana ball
and serve with a straw.

Illusion

4–6 ice cubes, plus extra
    to serve
2 measures vodka
½ measure Midori
½ measure Triple Sec
½ measure lime juice
lemonade, to top up
melon slices, to decorate
lemon slices, to decorate
cherries, to decorate

Put the ice cubes with the
vodka, Midori, Triple Sec and
lime juice into a cocktail
shaker and shake well. Put
more ice cubes into a large
hurricane glass and strain the
cocktail over the ice. Top up
with lemonade, stir and
decorate with melon and lemon
slices and cherries impaled
on a cocktail stick. Serve with
long straws.

Machete

ice cubes
1 measure vodka
2 measures pineapple juice
3 measures tonic water

Fill a tall glass or wine glass
with ice cubes. Pour the vodka,
pineapple juice and tonic water
into a mixing glass. Stir, then
pour over the ice cubes in the
tall or wine glass.

Fragrance

4–6 ice cubes, plus crushed
  ice to serve
1½ measures vodka
½ measure Midori
1 measure lemon juice
1 measure pineapple juice
1 dash sugar syrup
1 lemon wedge

Put the ice cubes with the
vodka, Midori, fruit juices and
sugar syrup into a cocktail
shaker and shake. Strain into a
highball glass filled with
crushed ice. Squeeze the lemon
wedge over the drink, drop it in
and serve with straws.

Green Island Quiet Sunday

4–6 ice cubes, plus crushed
  ice to serve
1 measure vodka
4 measures orange juice
3 dashes Amaretto di
  Saronno
few drops of grenadine

Put the ice cubes with the
vodka, orange juice and
Amaretto into a cocktail
shaker and shake well. Strain
into a highball glass filled with
crushed ice, then add a few
drops of grenadine.

Moscow Mule

6–8 ice cubes, cracked
2 measures vodka
juice of 2 limes
ginger beer, to top up
lime slice, to decorate
lime rind spiral, to decorate

Put the cracked ice into a
highball glass. Add the vodka
and lime juice, stir and top with
ginger beer. Decorate with a
lime slice and a lime rind spiral.

Lemon Grass Collins

crushed ice
2 measures lemon grass
  vodka
½ measure vanilla liqueur
1 dash lemon juice
1 dash sugar syrup
ginger beer, to top up
lemon slices, to decorate

Fill a large Collins glass with
crushed ice. Pour, one by one,
in order, the vodka, vanilla
liqueur, lemon juice and sugar
syrup over the ice. Stir, add
more ice and top up with
ginger beer. Decorate with
lemon slices and serve with
long straws.

Harvey Wallbanger

ice cubes
1 measure vodka
3 measures orange juice
1 teaspoon Galliano
orange slices, to decorate

Put some ice cubes into a
cocktail shaker and pour
the vodka and orange juice
over the ice. Shake well for
about 10 seconds, then strain
into a highball glass filled
with ice cubes. Float the
Galliano on top. Decorate with
orange slices.

Did you know?
A popular cocktail from the
1960s, the Harvey Wallbanger
is supposedly named after a
Californian surfer called Harvey,
who drank so many Screwdrivers
topped with Galliano (the Italian
herb liqueur) that as he left the bar
he banged and bounced from one
wall to the other.

Murray Hearn

ice cubes
1 ½ measures vodka
3 measures orange juice
½ measure Galliano
½ measure Cointreau
1 measure single cream
orange slice, to decorate

Put some ice cubes ino a
cocktail shaker and add the
vodka, orange juice, Galliano,
Cointreau and cream. Shake
well, then strain into a highball
glass filled with ice cubes.
Decorate with an orange slice.

One of Those

1 measure vodka
4 measures cranberry juice
2 dashes Amaretto di
   Saronno
juice of ½ lime
ice cubes
lime slice, to decorate

Pour the vodka, cranberry juice, Amaretto and lime juice into a cocktail shaker and shake well. Pour into a highball glass half-filled with ice cubes and decorate with a lime slice.

Sea Breeze

ice cubes
2 measures vodka
4 measures cranberry juice
2 measures pink
   grapefruit juice
2 lime wedges

Fill a highball glass with ice cubes. Pour the vodka and fruit juices over the ice. Squeeze over the lime wedges and stir lightly.

Cape Codder

ice cubes
2 measures vodka
4 measures cranberry juice
6 lime wedges

Fill a highball glass with ice cubes. Pour the vodka and cranberry juice over the ice. Squeeze 3 of the lime wedges into the drink. Stir well, decorate with the remaining lime wedges and serve with a straw.

Did you know?
This is a long drink similar to the Sea Breeze and currently one of the most popular cocktails around, thanks to the recent vogue for cranberry juice. Cape Cod in Massachusetts is responsible for much of the cranberry production in the United States.

Bay Breeze

ice cubes
4 measures cranberry juice
2 measures vodka
2 measures pineapple juice
lime wedges, to decorate

Fill a highball glass with ice
cubes and pour in the
cranberry juice. Pour the vodka
and pineapple juice into a
chilled cocktail shaker. Shake
well, then pour gently over the
cranberry juice. Decorate with
lime wedges and serve with
long straws.

Sex on the Beach

ice cubes
1 measure vodka
1 measure peach schnapps
1 measure cranberry juice
1 measure orange juice
1 measure pineapple juice
   (optional)
orange and lime slices,
   to decorate

Put some ice cubes into a
cocktail shaker and add the
vodka, schnapps, cranberry
juice, orange juice and
pineapple juice, if using. Shake
well. Pour over 3–4 ice cubes in
a tall glass, decorate with the
orange and lime slices and
serve with straws.

Did you know?
Peach schnapps, a strong dry spirit
produced by the distillation of
peaches, adds a peachy lift to a
number of fruity cocktails.

Sex in the Dunes

ice cubes
1 measure vodka
1 measure peach schnapps
½ measure Chambord
1 measure pineapple juice
pineapple strips, to
   decorate

Put some ice cubes into a
cocktail shaker with the vodka,
schnapps, Chambord and
pineapple juice. Shake until a
frost forms. Strain into an old-
fashioned glass filled with ice
cubes and decorate with
pineapple strips.

Parrot's Head Punch

ice cubes
1½ measures vodka
1 measure passion fruit
   liqueur
2 measures watermelon
   juice
1 measure cranberry juice
1½ measures pink
   grapefruit juice
grapefruit slices, to decorate

Fill a hurricane glass with ice cubes. Pour the ingredients, one by one in order over the ice. Decorate with grapefruit slices. Serve with long straws.

Basil's Mango Sling

ice cubes, plus crushed ice
1½ measures vodka
1½ measures mango purée
1 measure apricot liqueur
½ measure lemon juice
1 dash sugar syrup
soda water, to top up
mango slices, to decorate

Put some ice cubes with the vodka, mango purée, apricot liqueur, lemon juice and syrup into a cocktail shaker and add some ice cubes and shake very briefly. Strain into a sling glass filled with crushed ice. Top up with soda water and decorate with mango slices.

White Russian

6 ice cubes, cracked
1 measure vodka
1 measure Tia Maria
1 measure milk or
   double cream

Put half the ice into a cocktail shaker and add the vodka, Tia Maria and milk or cream. Shake until a frost forms. Put the remaining ice in a tall, narrow glass and strain the cocktail over the ice.

PDQ

4–5 ice cubes
1½ measures chilli-
    flavoured vodka
1 measure vodka
2 measures chilled
    beef stock
1 tablespoon fresh
    lemon juice
1 dash Tabasco sauce
1 dash Worcestershire
    sauce
salt and black pepper
lemon slice, to decorate
chilli, to decorate

Put the ice cubes into a cocktail
shaker. Pour the vodkas, stock,
lemon juice, Tabasco and
Worcestershire sauces over the
ice. Shake until a frost forms.
Strain into a hurricane glass.
Season to taste with salt and
pepper and decorate with a
lemon slice and a chilli.

Plasma

ice cubes
2 measures Absolut
    Peppar vodka
4 measures tomato juice
juice of ¼ lemon
2 dashes Tabasco sauce
4 dashes Worcestershire
    sauce
pinch of celery salt
pinch of black pepper
½ teaspoon Dijon mustard
1 teaspoon finely
    chopped dill
cucumber strip and
    seasoned split cherry
    tomato, to decorate

Put some ice cubes with all the
other ingredients into a shaker.
Shake vigorously but briefly,
then strain into a highball glass
over 6–8 ice cubes. Decorate
with a cucumber strip and a
seasoned split cherry tomato.

Did you know?
The flavoured vodka in the above
drink gives a heavily spiced base,
so add your Tabasco with care!

Bloody Mary

4–5 ice cubes
juice of ½ lemon
½ teaspoon horseradish
    sauce
2 drops Worcestershire
    sauce
1 drop Tabasco sauce
2 measures thick
    tomato juice
2 measures vodka
pinch of salt
pinch of cayenne pepper
celery stick, with the leaves
    left on, to decorate
lemon or lime slice,
    to decorate

Put the ice cubes into a cocktail
shaker. Pour the lemon juice,
horseradish, Worcestershire and
Tabasco sauces, tomato juice
and vodka over the ice. Shake
until a frost forms. Pour into a
tall glass and add the salt and
cayenne pepper. Decorate
with a celery stick.

Bloody Mary ▶

October Revolution

5–6 ice cubes, cracked
1 measure vodka
1 measure Tia Maria
1 measure crème de cacao
1 measure double cream

Put half the cracked ice into a cocktail shaker. Pour the vodka, Tia Maria, crème de cacao and cream over the ice and shake until a frost forms. Put the remaining ice into a tall, narrow glass, strain the cocktail over the ice and serve with a straw.

Le Mans

2–3 ice cubes, cracked
1 measure Cointreau
½ measure vodka
soda water, to top up
lemon slice, to decorate

Put the cracked ice into a tall glass. Add the Cointreau and vodka, stir and top up with soda water. Float a lemon slice on top of the drink to decorate.

Blue Moon

5–6 ice cubes, cracked
¾ measure vodka
¾ measure tequila
1 measure blue Curaçao
lemonade, to top up

Put half the cracked ice into a mixing glass. Add the vodka, tequila and blue Curaçao and stir to mix. Put the remaining ice into a tall glass and strain in the cocktail. Top up with lemonade and serve with a straw.

Hair Raiser

1–2 ice cubes, cracked
1 measure vodka
1 measure sweet vermouth
1 measure tonic water
lemon and lime rind spirals,
    to decorate

Put the cracked ice into a tall
glass and pour over the vodka,
vermouth and tonic water. Stir
lightly. Decorate with the lemon
and lime rind spirals and serve
with a straw.

Did you know?
You can make cracked ice by
putting some ice cubes into a strong
polythene bag and hitting the bag
with a rolling pin.

Screwdriver

2–3 ice cubes
1 ½ measures vodka
freshly squeezed orange
    juice, to top up

Put the ice cubes into a tumbler
and pour over the vodka.
Top up with orange juice
and stir lightly.

Marguerite

4–5 ice cubes, plus cracked
    ice to serve
3 measures vodka
juice of 1 lemon
juice of ½ orange
raspberry syrup,
    maraschino liqueur or
    grenadine, to taste

Put the ice cubes into a cocktail
shaker. Pour the vodka, fruit
juices and raspberry syrup,
maraschino liqueur or
grenadine over the ice. Shake
until a frost forms. Strain into
an old-fashioned glass filled
with cracked ice.

New Day

4–5 ice cubes
3 measures vodka
1 measure Calvados
1 measure apricot brandy
juice of ½ orange

Put the ice cubes into a cocktail shaker. Pour the vodka, Calvados, apricot brandy and orange juice over the ice. Shake until a frost forms. Strain into a sour glass.

Astronaut

8–10 ice cubes, cracked
½ measure white rum
½ measure vodka
½ measure fresh lemon juice
1 dash passion fruit juice
lemon wedge, to decorate

Put half the cracked ice in a cocktail shaker and add the rum, vodka and juices. Shake until a frost forms. Strain it into an old-fashioned glass filled with the remaining ice. Decorate with a lemon wedge.

Vodka Collins

6 ice cubes
2 measures vodka
juice of 1 lime
1 teaspoon caster sugar
soda water, to top up
lemon or lime slice, to decorate
cocktail cherry, to decorate

Put half the ice cubes into a cocktail shaker and add the vodka, lime juice and sugar. Shake until a frost forms. Strain into a large tumbler, add the remaining ice and top up with soda water. Decorate with a lemon or lime slice and a cherry.

Did you know?
Cocktail cherries, also called maraschino cherries, are stoned cherries preserved in a sugar syrup. The red variety come in a maraschino liqueur-flavoured syrup, which is slightly almondy, while the green kind are steeped in a minty crème de menthe-laced syrup.

Surf Rider

4–5 ice cubes
3 measures vodka
1 measure sweet vermouth
juice of ½ lemon
juice of 1 orange
½ teaspoon grenadine

Put the ice cubes into a cocktail shaker. Pour the vodka, vermouth, fruit juices and grenadine over the ice. Shake until a frost forms. Strain and pour into a sour glass.

Swallow Dive

ice cubes, plus crushed ice
    to serve
1 measure honey vodka
1 measure Chambord
1 measure lime juice
4 raspberries, plus 2
    to decorate

Put some ice cubes with all the other ingredients into a cocktail shaker. Shake well. Strain over crushed ice in an old-fashioned glass. Top up with more crushed ice and decorate with the 2 extra raspberries.

Tokyo Joe

ice cubes
1 measure vodka
1 measure Midori

Put some ice cubes into a cocktail shaker, add the vodka and Midori and shake well. Strain into an old-fashioned glass, over ice cubes if you like.

White Leopard

4–5 ice cubes
2 measures vodka
1 measure Grand Marnier
juice of ½ orange
juice of ½ lemon

Put the ice cubes into a cocktail shaker. Pour the vodka, Grand Marnier and fruit juices over the ice. Shake until a frost forms. Strain into a sour glass.

Did you know?

Grand Marnier is the most well known of the orange-flavoured liqueurs. Created in France in the late nineteenth century, its golden colour indicates its brandy base and its unique tang comes from bitter tropical oranges. It comes in two varieties – Cordon Rouge and Cordon Jaune, the former being both the best quality and the strongest.

Black Russian

ice cubes, cracked
2 measures vodka
1 measure Kahlúa
chocolate stick, to decorate (optional)

Put some cracked ice into a mixing glass. Add the vodka and Kahlúa and stir. Pour into a short glass without straining. Decorate with a chocolate stick, if you like.

Mudslide

10 ice cubes, cracked
1 measure vodka
1 measure Kahlúa
1 measure Baileys Irish Cream

Put 6 of the cracked ice cubes into a cocktail shaker and add the vodka, Kahlúa and Baileys. Shake until a frost forms. Strain into a tumbler and add the remaining cracked ice.

Godmother

2–3 ice cubes, cracked
1½ measures vodka
½ measure Amaretto
  di Saronno

Put the cracked ice into a
tumbler. Add the vodka and
Amaretto and stir lightly.

Did you know?
To make a Godchild, shake
1 measure each of vodka, Amaretto
and double cream with ice. Strain
into a cocktail glass and serve.

Snapdragon

ice cubes
2 measures vodka
4 measures green crème
  de menthe
soda water, to top up
mint sprig, to decorate

Fill a highball glass with ice
cubes. Pour the vodka and
crème de menthe over the ice
and stir. Top up with soda water.
Decorate with a mint sprig.

St Petersburg

ice cubes
1 measure vodka
½ measure Chartreuse

Put the ice cubes into a cocktail
shaker and pour over the vodka
and Chartreuse. Shake well,
then pour into a cocktail glass.

Iceberg

4–6 ice cubes
1½ measures vodka
1 dash Pernod

Put the ice cubes into an old-fashioned glass. Pour the vodka over the ice and add the Pernod.

Vodka Sazerac

1 sugar cube
2 drops Angostura bitters
3 drops Pernod
2–3 ice cubes
2 measures vodka
lemonade, to top up

Put the sugar cube in an old-fashioned glass and shake the bitters on to it. Add the Pernod and swirl it around to coat the inside of the glass. Drop in the ice cubes and pour in the vodka. Top up with lemonade and stir gently.

Gingersnap

2–3 ice cubes
3 measures vodka
1 measure ginger wine
soda water, to top up

Combine the vodka, ginger wine and ice in an old-fashioned glass and stir gently. Top up with soda water.

Herbert Lee

4–5 ice cubes
2 measures vodka
1 measure Calvados
1 teaspoon crème de cassis

Put the ice cubes into a mixing glass. Pour the vodka, Calvados and crème de cassis over the ice. Stir vigorously, then strain into a chilled cocktail glass.

Did you know?
You can make a Davey-Davey by replacing the crème de cassis with the juice of ½ grapefruit.

Haven

ice cubes
1 tablespoon grenadine
1 measure Pernod
1 measure vodka
soda water, to top up

Put 2–3 ice cubes in an old-fashioned glass. Dash the grenadine over the ice, then pour in the Pernod and vodka. Top up with soda water.

French Leave

ice cubes
1 measure orange juice
1 measure vodka
1 measure Pernod

Put some ice cubes with all the other ingredients into a cocktail shaker and shake well. Strain into a cocktail glass.

Federation

4–5 ice cubes
3 drops orange or
    Angostura bitters
2 measures vodka
1 measure port

Put the ice cubes into a mixing glass. Shake the bitters over the ice. Add the vodka and port. Stir vigorously and strain into a chilled cocktail glass.

Katinka

ice cubes
1½ measures vodka
1 measure apricot brandy
2 teaspoons fresh lime juice
mint sprig, to decorate

Put some ice cubes and all the other ingredients into a cocktail shaker and shake well. Strain into a cocktail glass and decorate with a mint sprig.

Goombay Smash

ice cubes
1½ measures coconut rum
1 measure Cachaça
½ measure apricot brandy
½ measure lime juice
4 measures pineapple juice
pineapple slices, lime rind
    twist and cocktail cherries,
    to decorate

Put some ice cubes with all the ingredients into a cocktail shaker and shake well. Strain over ice into a large glass. Decorate with pineapple slices, a lime rind twist and cherries impaled on a cocktail stick.

Did you know?

An unprepossessing, sky-blue building in Green Turtle Bay is the birthplace of the legendary Goombay Smash. The drink's inventor, the late Miss Emily Cooper, never partook of the cocktail herself because of her Christian beliefs, but that didn't stop her from running one of the most popular drinking posts in the Bahamas. Miss Emily passed on her secret recipe for Goombay Smash to her daughter, so you'll have to travel to the Blue Bee to try the genuine article.

Goombay Smash ▶

Leolin

4–5 ice cubes
3 measures vodka
1 measure apricot brandy
juice of 1 lime or lemon
2 drops Peychaud or
    Angostura bitters

Put the ice cubes into a mixing
glass. Pour the vodka, apricot
brandy, fruit juice and bitters
over the ice. Stir vigorously
and strain into a chilled
cocktail glass.

Flower Power Sour

ice cubes
1½ measures Absolut
    Mandarin vodka
½ measure Mandarine
    Napoléon
2 teaspoons elderflower
    cordial
2 teaspoons sugar syrup
1 measure fresh lemon juice
orange rind, to decorate

Put some ice cubes with the
vodka, Mandarine Napoléon,
elderflower cordial, sugar syrup
and lemon juice into a cocktail
shaker and shake well. Strain
into an old-fashioned glass
filled with ice cubes and
decorate with orange rind.

Road Runner

6 ice cubes, cracked
2 measures vodka
1 measure Amaretto
    di Saronno
1 measure coconut milk
grated nutmeg, to decorate

Put the cracked ice into a
cocktail shaker and add the
vodka, Amaretto and coconut
milk. Shake until a frost forms,
then strain into a cocktail glass.
Sprinkle with a pinch of freshly
grated nutmeg.

Rising Sun

ice cubes
2 measures vodka
2 teaspoons passion fruit
    syrup
3 measures grapefruit juice
pink grapefruit slice, to
    decorate

Put some of the ice cubes with
the vodka, passion fruit syrup
and grapefruit juice into a
shaker and shake to mix. Strain
into an old-fashioned glass over
6–8 ice cubes. Decorate with a
pink grapefruit slice.

Cool Wind

4–5 ice cubes
1 measure dry vermouth
½ teaspoon Cointreau
3 measures vodka
juice of ½ grapefruit

Put the ice cubes into a mixing
glass. Pour the vermouth,
Cointreau, vodka and grapefruit
juice over the ice. Stir gently,
then strain into a chilled
cocktail glass.

Warsaw Cocktail

6 ice cubes
1 measure vodka
½ measure blackberry-
    flavoured brandy
½ measure dry vermouth
1 teaspoon fresh lemon
    juice

Put the ice cubes into a cocktail
shaker and add the vodka,
brandy, vermouth and lemon
juice. Shake until a frost forms.
Strain into a cocktail glass.

Yokohama

4–5 ice cubes
3 measures vodka
3 drops Pernod
juice of 1 orange
½ teaspoon grenadine

Put the ice cubes into a cocktail shaker. Pour the vodka, Pernod, orange juice and grenadine over the ice. Shake until a frost forms. Strain and pour into a chilled cocktail glass.

Xantippe

4–5 ice cubes
1 measure cherry brandy
1 measure yellow
   Chartreuse
2 measures vodka

Put the ice cubes into a mixing glass. Pour the cherry brandy, Chartreuse and vodka over the ice and stir vigorously. Strain into a chilled cocktail glass.

Scotch Frog

ice cubes
2 measures vodka
1 measure Galliano
1 measure Cointreau
juice of 1 lime
1 dash Angostura bitters
2 dashes maraschino
   cherry syrup

Fill a cocktail shaker three-quarters full with ice cubes. Add all the other ingredients, shake well and strain into a chilled cocktail glass.

Did you know?
Named after Major Giuseppe Galliáno, an Italian military hero, Galliano is a sweet golden-yellow liqueur with a wonderfully herbal flavour, including distinct aniseed overtones. As a bonus it comes in a highly attractive, tall bottle.

White Spider

2 measures vodka
1 measure clear crème
    de menthe
crushed ice (optional)

Pour the vodka and crème de
menthe into a cocktail shaker.
Shake well, then pour into a
chilled cocktail glass or over
crushed ice.

Inspiration

4–5 ice cubes
½ measure Bénédictine
½ measure dry vermouth
2 measures vodka
lime rind spiral, to decorate

Put the ice cubes into a mixing
glass. Pour the Bénédictine,
vermouth and vodka over
the ice. Stir vigorously, then
strain into a chilled cocktail
glass and decorate with the
lime rind spiral.

Combined Forces

4–5 ice cubes
2 measures vodka
1 measure dry vermouth
½ teaspoon Triple Sec
juice of ½ fresh lemon

Put the ice cubes into a
mixing glass. Add all the other
ingredients, stir vigorously
then strain into a chilled
cocktail glass.

vodka 63

Vodka Gibson

6 ice cubes
1 measure vodka
½ measure dry vermouth
pearl onion, to garnish
   (optional)

Put the ice cubes into a cocktail
shaker and add the vodka and
vermouth. Shake until a frost
forms, then strain into a
cocktail glass and decorate
with a pearl onion impaled
on a cocktail stick.

Vanilla Skyy

ice cubes
2 teaspoons dry vermouth
1 measure vanilla-infused
   vodka (Stoli Vanil)
1 measure Skyy vodka
½ measure apple schnapps
apple chunks frozen in
   apple juice ice cubes,
   to decorate

Fill a mixing glass with ice
cubes. Add the vermouth, stir
and strain, discarding the
excess vermouth and leaving
the flavoured ice. Add the
vodkas and the schnapps,
stir, then strain into a chilled
cocktail glass. Decorate with
apple-chunk ice cubes.

Did you know?
With hints of apple and vanilla,
Skyy is an American vodka of
exceptional purity.

Iced Lemon and Mint Vodka

1 tablespoon lemon juice
1 measure lemon cordial
1 measure chilled vodka
ice cubes
tonic water, to top up
mint sprigs, to decorate

Pour the lemon juice, lemon
cordial and vodka into a
cocktail shaker and shake well.
Pour into a tall glass half-filled
with ice cubes. Top up with
tonic water, add the mint sprigs
and serve immediately.

Vesper

ice cubes
3 measures gin
1 measure vodka
½ measure Lillet
lemon rind twist,
    to decorate

Put the ice cubes with the gin, vodka and Lillet into a cocktail shaker and shake well. Strain into a chilled cocktail glass and add a lemon rind twist.

Did you know?
This cocktail, made with a combination of gin and vodka, is prepared by James Bond's renowned method; in other words it is shaken, not stirred. Lillet is a blend of wine and brandy, flavoured with fruit and herbs, made in France.

Cosmopolitan

ice cubes
1½ measures citron vodka
1 measure Cointreau
1½ measures cranberry
    juice
¼ measure fresh lime juice
orange rind twist, flamed
    (see page 189)

Put the ice cubes into a cocktail shaker, add the vodka, Cointreau, cranberry juice and lime juice and shake well. Strain into a chilled cocktail glass and add a flamed orange rind twist.

Parson's Nose

2 measures vodka
½ measure Amaretto
½ measure crème de peche
1 measure Angostura
    bitters

Stir the ingredients in a mixing glass, then strain into a chilled Martini glass and serve.

Vodkatini

¼ measure dry vermouth
3 measures frozen vodka
1 green olive or lemon
    rind twist

Swirl the vermouth around a
chilled Martini glass, then pour
in the vodka. Finish by adding
the olive or a lemon rind twist.

White Elephant

ice cubes
1½ measures vodka
1 measure white crème
    de cacao
1 measure single cream
½ measure full-cream milk

Put the ice cubes into a cocktail
shaker, add the vodka, crème de
cacao, cream and milk and
shake well. Strain into a chilled
Martini glass.

Did you know?
A real heavyweight, the White
Elephant is a seriously sumptuous
concoction, but the vodka perfectly
offsets the richness of its creamy
contents.

Polish Martini

ice cubes
1 measure Zubrowka vodka
1 measure Krupnik vodka
1 measure Wyborowa vodka
1 measure apple juice
lemon rind twist, to
    decorate

Put the ice cubes into a mixing
glass. Pour in the vodkas
and the apple juice and stir
well. Strain into a chilled
cocktail glass and add a lemon
rind twist.

Chocotini

cocoa powder
ice cubes
2 measures vodka
1 measure dark crème
   de cacao
¼ measure sugar syrup
½ measure chocolate syrup

Frost a chilled Martini glass by dipping into water, then pressing into cocoa powder. Put the ice cubes into a cocktail shaker, add the vodka, crème de cacao, sugar syrup and chocolate syrup and shake well. Strain into the prepared glass.

Decatini

ice cubes
2 measures raspberry
   vodka
½ measure chocolate syrup,
   plus extra to decorate
1 measure morello cherry
   purée
½ measure double cream

Fill a cocktail shaker with ice cubes and add the vodka, chocolate syrup and half the cream. Shake well and strain into a chilled Martini glass. Shake the cherry purée with the remaining cream in a clean shaker. Slowly pour the cherry liquid on to a spoon that is held in contact with the chocolate liquid in the glass; this will produce a layering effect. Decorate with a 'swirl' of chocolate syrup.

Lemon Martini

ice cubes
1½ measures citron vodka
1 measure fresh lemon juice
¼ measure sugar syrup
¼ measure Cointreau
3 drops orange bitters
orange rind twist,
   to decorate

Put the ice cubes with the vodka, lemon juice, sugar syrup, Cointreau and bitters into a cocktail shaker and shake well. Strain into a chilled Martini glass and add an orange rind twist.

Blackberry Martini

2 measures Absolut Kurant
  vodka
1 measure crème de mure
ice cubes
blackberry, to decorate

Put the vodka and crème de mure into a mixing glass, add some ice cubes and stir well. Strain into a chilled Martini glass and decorate with a single blackberry.

Apple Martini

ice cubes
2 measures vodka
1 measure apple schnapps
1 tablespoon apple purée
1 dash lime juice
pinch of ground cinnamon
red apple wedges, to
  decorate

Put some ice cubes with the vodka, schnapps, apple purée, lime juice and cinnamon into a cocktail shaker and shake well. Double strain into a chilled Martini glass. Decorate with red apple wedges.

Vodka Sour

4–5 ice cubes
2 measures vodka
½ measure sugar syrup
1 egg white
1½ measures fresh lemon
  juice
3 drops Angostura bitters,
  to decorate

Put the ice cubes into a cocktail shaker, add the vodka, sugar syrup, egg white and lemon juice and shake until a frost forms. Pour without straining into a cocktail glass and shake the Angostura bitters on the top to decorate.

Bellini-tini

2 measures vodka
½ measure peach schnapps
2 teaspoons peach juice
Champagne, to top up
peach slices, to decorate

Put the vodka, schnapps and peach juice into a cocktail shaker and shake well. Pour into a cocktail glass and top up with Champagne. Decorate with peach slices.

Horizon

ice cubes
1½ measures Zubrowka Bison Grass vodka
½ measure Xante pear liqueur
1 measure pressed apple juice
1 teaspoon passion fruit liqueur
1 dash lemon juice
lemon rind twist, to decorate

Put some ice cubes with all the ingredients into a cocktail shaker and shake well. Double strain into a chilled Martini glass. Decorate with a lemon rind twist.

Valentine Martini

ice cubes
2 measures raspberry vodka
6 raspberries, plus 2 to decorate
½ measure lime juice
1 dash sugar syrup
lime rind twist, to decorate

Put some ice cubes with the vodka, raspberries, lime juice and sugar syrup into a cocktail shaker and shake well. Double strain into a chilled Martini glass. Decorate with the extra raspberries impaled on a cocktail stick and a lime rind twist.

Did you know?

Sugar syrup is used in many cocktails – it blends more quickly into cold liquids than ordinary sugar. It is easy to make your own. Put equal quantities of granulated sugar and water into a saucepan and bring slowly to the boil, stirring until the sugar has dissolved. Then boil, without stirring, for 1–2 minutes. Leave to cool, then store in a sterilized bottle. It will keep for up to 2 months in the refrigerator.

The Glamour Martini

ice cubes
1½ measures vodka
½ measure cherry brandy
2 measures blood orange
    juice
½ measure lime juice
orange rind twist, to
    decorate

Put some ice cubes with all
the other ingredients into a
cocktail shaker and shake well.
Strain into a chilled Martini
glass. Decorate with an orange
rind twist.

Did you know?
The Glamour Martini is a signature
drink of the Glamour Bar in
Shanghai, where an extensive,
leather-bound list of classic and
contemporary cocktails sits on top
of the gleaming metal bar.

Kurant Blush

ice cubes
1½ measures Absolut
    Kurant vodka
½ measure fraise liqueur
1 measure cranberry juice
2 lime wedges
redcurrant, to decorate

Put some ice cubes with all the
other ingredients in a cocktail
shaker and shake well. Double
strain into a chilled Martini
glass and decorate with a
redcurrant impaled on a
cocktail stick.

Watermelon Martini

ice cubes
1 lime wedge
4 watermelon chunks
1½ measures vodka
½ measure passion
    fruit liqueur
1 dash cranberry juice
watermelon wedge,
    to decorate

Squeeze the lime wedge into a
cocktail shaker, add some ice
cubes, the watermelon chunks,
vodka, passion fruit liqueur and
cranberry juice and shake well.
Double strain into a chilled
Martini glass and decorate
with a watermelon wedge
impaled on a cocktail stick.

Watermelon Martini ▶

Dragon's Fire

ice cubes
1½ measures Absolut
   Mandarin vodka
1 measure Cointreau
1 dash lime juice
1 measure cranberry juice
orange rind twist, to
   decorate

Put some ice cubes with the
vodka, Cointreau and fruit
juices into a cocktail shaker and
shake well. Double strain into a
chilled Martini glass. Decorate
with an orange rind twist.

Naked Vodkatini

3 measures frozen
   Stolichnaya vodka
½ measure Noilly Prat
olives, to decorate

Stir the vodka and Noilly Prat
together in a mixing glass, then
strain into a chilled Martini
glass. Decorate with olives.

Absolut Wonder

lemon wedge
grated chocolate
3 measures Absolut Vanilla
   vodka
1 measure Mozart white
   chocolate liqueur
cocktail cherry, to decorate

Frost the rim of a chilled
Martini glass with the lemon
wedge, then press into the
grated chocolate. Pour the
vodka and liqueur into a
chilled cocktail shaker and
shake well. Double strain into
the prepared glass. Finally, drop
a cherry into the bottom of the
glass, to decorate.

Did you know?
The Absolut range of vodkas
encompasses all kinds of fruit
flavours, including Mandarin, Citron
and Raspberry, as well as herbs and
spices, such as Vanilla featured in
the cocktail above and Peppar,
flavoured with jalapeño chillies.

Razzmopolitan

1½ measures Stoli Razberi
1 measure Cointreau
1 dash lime juice
1 measure cranberry juice
4 raspberries, plus
   2 to decorate

Put the vodka, Cointreau, fruit juices and raspberries into a cocktail shaker and shake well. Double strain into a chilled Martini glass and decorate with the extra raspberries impaled on a cocktail stick.

Laila Cocktail

2 lime wedges
2 strawberries, hulled
4 blueberries, plus 3
   to decorate
1 dash mango purée
2 measures raspberry
   vodka
ice cubes

Muddle the lime wedges, berries and mango purée in a cocktail shaker. Add the vodka with some ice cubes and shake vigorously. Double strain into a chilled Martini glass and garnish with the extra blueberries impaled on a cocktail stick.

Dark Knight

ice cubes
1 measure Kahlúa
1 measure vodka
1 measure cold espresso
   coffee
2 teaspoons sugar syrup

Put some ice cubes with the Kahlúa, vodka, coffee and sugar syrup into a cocktail shaker and shake well. Strain into a chilled Martini glass and serve.

Red Star Alexander

ice cubes
1 measure vodka
1 measure Kahlúa
1 measure dark crème
   de cacao
1 measure single cream
grated nutmeg, to decorate

Put some ice cubes with the
vodka, Kahlúa, dark crème de
cacao and cream into a cocktail
shaker and shake to mix. Strain
into a chilled cocktail glass and
sprinkle with nutmeg.

Did you know?

The dark crème de cacao and
nutmeg decoration in Red Star
Alexander give a deliciously rich
twist to the classic White Russian
(see page 47).

Diamond Ring

1 dash boiling water
1 teaspoon clear honey
3 basil leaves
1½ measures Zubrowka
   Bison Grass vodka
1 measure pressed
   apple juice
ice cubes
apple slices, to decorate

Stir the hot water, honey and
basil leaves together in a
cocktail shaker until well
blended. Add the vodka, apple
juice and some ice cubes. Shake
well and double strain into a
chilled Martini glass. Decorate
with apple slices.

Storm at Sea

8–10 ice cubes
2 measures cranberry juice
1 measure pineapple juice
2 teaspoons elderflower
   cordial
1½ measures Blavod vodka

Put half the ice cubes with the
fruit juices and elderflower
cordial into a cocktail shaker
and shake well. Strain into an
old-fashioned glass over the
remaining ice cubes. Slowly add
the vodka – it will separate
briefly. Serve immediately.

Raft

1 measure vodka
1 measure bitter lemon

Pour the vodka into a tumbler,
then pour in the bitter lemon.
Cover the top of the glass with
the palm of your hand to seal
the contents inside and grip it
with your fingers. Slam it down
on a surface 3 times, then gulp
it down.

Vocachino

ice cubes
2 measures vodka
½ measure Kahlúa
½ measure cold espresso
    coffee
½ measure single cream
1 dash sugar syrup
½ teaspoon cocoa powder

Put the ice cubes into a cocktail
shaker and add the vodka,
Kahlúa, coffee, cream, sugar
syrup and cocoa powder. Shake
briefly then strain into
4 shot glasses.

Kamikaze

6 ice cubes, cracked
½ measure vodka
½ measure Curaçao
½ measure lime juice

Put the cracked ice into a
cocktail shaker and add the
vodka, Curaçao and lime juice.
Shake until a frost forms, then
strain into a shot glass.

Lemon Drop

ice cubes
¾ measure lemon vodka
¾ measure Limoncello
1 dash fresh lemon juice
1 dash lime cordial

Put some ice cubes with all the other ingredients into a cocktail shaker and shake briefly. Strain into a shot glass.

Legal High

1 dash Amaretto
1 pink grapefruit wedge
1 measure Vod-Ca (hemp vodka)
ice cubes

Muddle the Amaretto and grapefruit in the base of a shaker. Add the vodka and a few ice cubes and shake briefly. Strain into a shot glass.

Purple Haze

ice cubes
1 measure vodka
1 dash Cointreau
1 dash fresh lemon juice
1 dash Chambord

Put some ice cubes with the vodka, Cointreau and lemon juice into a cocktail shaker and shake briefly. Strain into a shot glass. Add the dash of Chambord slowly at the end: this will settle towards the bottom of the drink.

Rock Chick

ice cubes
1 measure Absolut
    Kurant vodka
1 dash peach schnapps
1 dash fresh lime juice

Put some ice cubes with all the
other ingredients into a cocktail
shaker and shake briefly. Strain
into a shot glass.

Strawberry Fields

1 lime wedge
1 dash strawberry syrup
1 strawberry, hulled
1 measure Absolut
    Kurant vodka
ice cubes

Muddle the lime wedge, syrup
and strawberry in a cocktail
shaker, add the vodka and some
ice cubes and shake briefly.
Strain into a shot glass.

Mint Zing Ting

1 lime wedge
2 mint leaves
1 dash sugar syrup
1 measure apple-soaked
    vodka
ice cubes
cucumber strip, to decorate

Muddle the lime wedge, mint
and sugar syrup in a cocktail
shaker, then add the vodka
and some ice cubes. Shake
briefly, then strain into a chilled
shot glass and decorate with a
cucumber strip.

Pillow Talk

½ measure chilled
   strawberry vodka
½ measure Mozart white
   chocolate liqueur
1 dash aerosol cream

Pour the chilled vodka into a
shot glass. Using the back of a
bar spoon, slowly float the
chocolate liqueur over the
vodka. Top with the cream.

Poppy

ice cubes
¾ measure vodka
1 dash Chambord
1 teaspoon pineapple purée

Put some ice cubes with all the
other ingredients into a cocktail
shaker and shake briefly. Strain
into a shot glass.

Chocolate Berry

ice cubes
1 measure raspberry-
   flavoured vodka
1 dash crème de cassis
1 dash Mozart dark
   chocolate liqueur
2 blueberries, to decorate
1 raspberry, to decorate

Put some ice cubes with all the
other ingredients into a cocktail
shaker and shake briefly. Strain
into a chilled shot glass. Impale
the berries on a cocktail stick
and eat after drinking the shot.

Did you know?
Treat your guests to a liquid dessert
with the above extravagant
combination of vodka, crème de
cassis and dark chocolate liqueur,
all rounded off with a miniature
berry kebab.

Jo nul

ice cubes
½ measure vodka
½ measure Chambord
½ measure Baileys
    Irish Cream
caster sugar
strawberry, to decorate

Put some ice cubes with the
vodka, Chambord and Baileys
into a cocktail shaker and shake
briefly. Frost the rim of a shot
glass by dipping into water,
then pressing into the sugar.
Strain the cocktail into the
prepared glass and serve with
a strawberry on the rim.

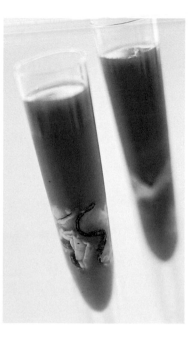

Oyster Shot

1 small, plump oyster
¾ measure chilled pepper
    vodka
¾ measure chilled tomato
    juice
3 drops Tabasco sauce
dash Worcestershire sauce
1 lime wedge, squeezed
pinch of freshly cracked
    black pepper
pinch of celery salt

In a large shot glass, add all the
ingredients in the above order,
then slowly tip the entire
contents down your throat.

Bloody Simple

1 measure chilled pepper
    (or chilli-infused) vodka
2–3 drops Tabasco sauce
½ teaspoon ground black
    pepper
½ teaspoon celery salt
tomato wedge

Pour the vodka into a shot
glass, then add the Tabasco
sauce. Combine the black
pepper and celery salt on
a small saucer and mix
thoroughly. Lightly coat
the tomato wedge in the
mixture, then eat it after
drinking the shot.

Gin

Gin was first distilled in Holland in the seventeenth century where it was called 'genever' by physician Franciscus de la Boe. Made from juniper berries, gin, like many spirits, was originally produced and sold as a medicine. However, it was soon being cheaply mass-produced for consumption as an intoxicating drink. Gin became popular with the poor because it was so cheap and offered an alcohol-induced release. Eventually, production had to be regulated and restricted because thousands of people became addicted to cheap gin, resulting in social and economic problems throughout England in the 1700s. It was during this time that the term 'mother's ruin' was coined, referring to the many poor women who became fatally addicted to the spirit. Against the odds, the image of gin wasn't entirely tarnished, and with licensing and production controls in place, gin became the favoured drink during the fashionable 1920s, when many new cocktails were created that are still drunk today.

Gin and Tonic

ice cubes
2 measures gin
4 measures tonic water
2 lime wedges, to decorate

Fill a highball glass with ice cubes, pour in the gin and then the tonic water. Decorate with lime wedges.

Albemarle Fizz

4–6 ice cubes
1 measure Tanqueray gin
juice of ½ lemon
2 dashes raspberry syrup
½ teaspoon sugar syrup
soda water, to top up
cocktail cherries, to
    decorate

Put half the ice cubes into a mixing glass and add the gin, lemon juice, raspberry and sugar syrups. Stir to mix, then strain into a highball glass. Add the remaining ice cubes and top up with soda water. Decorate with two cherries impaled on a cocktail stick and serve with straws.

Did you know?

Tanqueray gin is made in London using a recipe created by Charles Tanqueray in the 1830s. It is renowned for its distinctively smooth, lingering taste.

Pink Camellia

ice cubes
2 measures gin
1 measure apricot brandy
2 measures orange juice
2 measures lemon juice
1 measure Campari
1 dash egg white

Fill a cocktail shaker three-quarters full with ice cubes. Add all the other ingredients, shake well, then strain into a chilled cocktail glass.

Tanqstream

ice cubes, cracked
2 measures Tanqueray gin
2 teaspoons fresh lime juice
3 measures soda water or
    tonic water
2 teaspoons crème de cassis
lime slices, to decorate
fresh berries, to decorate

Put some cracked ice with the gin and lime juice into a cocktail shaker and shake to mix. Strain into a highball glass half-filled with cracked ice. For a dry Tanqstream, add soda water; for a less dry drink, add tonic water. Stir in the cassis and decorate with the lime slices and fresh berries.

Golden Dawn

4–5 ice cubes
juice of ½ orange
1 measure Calvados
1 measure apricot brandy
3 measures gin
soda water, to top up
orange rind strip,
    to decorate

Put the ice cubes into a cocktail shaker and pour over the orange juice, Calvados, apricot brandy and gin. Shake until a frost forms. Strain into a highball glass, top up with soda water and decorate with an orange rind strip.

Sweet Sixteen

6–8 ice cubes
2 measures gin
juice of ½ lime
2 dashes grenadine
1 teaspoon sugar syrup
bitter lemon, to top up
lemon rind strip, to decorate

Put half the ice cubes into a cocktail shaker and pour over the gin, lime juice, grenadine and sugar syrup. Shake until a frost forms. Put the remaining ice into a highball glass, strain the cocktail over the ice and top up with bitter lemon. Decorate with a lemon rind strip.

Did you know?
Quinine helps to give an edge to the flavour of bitter lemon so that it is not over-sweet. In fact, quinine is a widely used flavouring in drinks, notably vermouth and tonic water, in the latter case contributing to the popularity of the G&T in Britain's tropical colonies as an anti-malarial tipple.

Tom Collins

2 measures gin
1½ teaspoons lemon juice
1 teaspoon sugar syrup
ice cubes
soda water, to top up
lemon slice, to decorate

Put the gin, lemon juice and sugar syrup into a tall glass, stir well and fill the glass with ice. Top up with soda water and decorate with a lemon slice.

Did you know?

Tom Collins is the best known of the Collins cocktails, a group of long drinks made popular during the First World War and served in a highball or Collins glass. Originally the Tom Collins was made with Old Tom, a slightly sweetened gin, but now it is made with dry gin. Variations on the Collins drink use different spirits: the John Collins uses whiskey, the Pierre Collins uses cognac, and the Pedro Collins uses rum.

Berry Collins

4 raspberries
4 blueberries
1 dash strawberry syrup
crushed ice
2 measures gin
2 teaspoons fresh lemon juice
sugar syrup, to taste
soda water, to top up
raspberries, blueberries and lemon slice, to decorate

Muddle the berries and strawberry syrup in a highball glass, then fill the glass with crushed ice. Add the gin, lemon juice and sugar syrup. Stir well, then top up with soda water. Decorate with raspberries, blueberries and a lemon slice.

Gin Fizz

ice cubes
2 measures Plymouth gin
1 measure fresh lemon juice
2–3 dashes sugar syrup
¼ beaten egg white
soda water, to top up
lemon slices and mint sprig, to decorate

Put some ice cubes with the gin, lemon juice, sugar syrup and egg white into a cocktail shaker and shake to mix. Strain into a highball glass and top up with soda water. Decorate with lemon slices and a mint sprig.

Horse's Neck

4–6 ice cubes
1½ measures gin
dry ginger ale, to top up
lemon rind spiral, to
    decorate

Put the ice cubes into a tall
glass and pour in the gin. Top
up with ginger ale, then dangle
the lemon rind spiral over the
edge of the glass.

Alice Springs

4–5 ice cubes
1 measure fresh lemon juice
1 measure fresh orange
    juice
½ teaspoon grenadine
3 measures gin
3 drops Angostura bitters
soda water, to top up
orange slice, to decorate

Put the ice cubes into a cocktail
shaker. Pour the fruit juices,
grenadine and gin over the ice.
Add the bitters and shake until
a frost forms. Pour into a tall
glass and top up with soda
water. Decorate with an orange
slice and serve with straws.

Gin Floradora

4–5 ice cubes
½ teaspoon sugar syrup
juice of ½ lime
½ teaspoon grenadine
2 measures gin
dry ginger ale, to top up
lime rind twist, to decorate

Put the ice cubes into a cocktail
shaker. Pour the sugar syrup,
lime juice, grenadine and gin
over the ice and shake until
a frost forms. Pour without
straining into a hurricane glass.
Top up with dry ginger ale and
decorate with a lime rind twist.

Cherry Julep

3–4 ice cubes, plus finely
    chopped ice to serve
juice of ½ lemon
1 teaspoon sugar syrup
1 teaspoon grenadine
1 measure cherry brandy
1 measure sloe gin
2 measures gin
lemon rind strips,
    to decorate

Put the ice cubes into a cocktail
shaker. Pour the lemon juice,
sugar syrup, grenadine, cherry
brandy, sloe gin and gin over
the ice. Shake until a frost
forms. Strain into a highball
glass filled with chopped ice
and decorate with lemon
rind strips.

Burnsides

8–10 ice cubes
2 drops Angostura bitters
1 teaspoon cherry brandy
1 measure sweet vermouth
2 measures dry vermouth
2 measures gin
lemon rind strips,
    to decorate

Put half the ice cubes into a
cocktail shaker. Dash the bitters
over the ice and add the cherry
brandy, vermouths and gin.
Shake lightly and strain over
the remaining ice cubes in a
highball glass. Decorate with
lemon rind strips.

Gin Sling

4–5 ice cubes
juice of ½ lemon
1 measure cherry brandy
3 measures gin
soda water, to top up
cocktail cherries, to
    decorate

Put the ice cubes into a cocktail
shaker. Pour the lemon juice,
cherry brandy and gin over the
ice. Shake until a frost forms.
Pour without straining into a
hurricane glass and top up
with soda water. Decorate with
cherries and serve with straws.

Did you know?
This cocktail is redolent of the long-
gone and highly privileged days of
colonialism – for some, at least –
when meeting at the club on a
warm summer's evening was the
invariable prelude to a fine dinner.

Singapore Sling

ice cubes
1 measure gin
½ measure cherry brandy
¼ measure Cointreau
¼ measure Bénédictine
½ measure grenadine
½ measure lime juice
5 measures pineapple juice
1 dash Angostura bitters
pineapple slice and cocktail
    cherry, to decorate

Put some ice cubes with all the
other ingredients into a cocktail
shaker and shake well. Strain
over ice cubes in a sling glass.
Decorate with a pineapple slice
and a cherry.

Orange Blossom

4 orange slices, plus extra to
    decorate
2 teaspoons almond syrup
crushed ice
2 measures gin
1 measure pink grapefruit
    juice
3 dashes Angostura bitters

Muddle the orange slices and
almond syrup in a highball
glass. Fill the glass with
crushed ice and pour in the gin.
Stir, top with the grapefruit
juice and bitters and decorate
with extra orange slices. Serve
with straws.

Zed

ice cubes, cracked
1 measure gin
1 measure Mandarine
    Napoléon
3 measures fresh pineapple
    juice
1 teaspoon sugar
1 lemon slice, cut in half,
    to decorate
mint sprig, to decorate

Put some cracked ice into a
cocktail shaker and pour over
the gin, Mandarine Napoléon,
pineapple juice and sugar.
Shake lightly to mix. Pour into
a tall glass and decorate with
lemon slice halves and mint
sprig on top.

Hong Kong Sling

ice cubes
1½ measures gin
½ measure lychee liqueur
1 measure lychee purée
1 measure lemon juice
½ measure sugar syrup
soda water, to top up
fresh lychee in its shell,
   to decorate

Put some ice cubes into a
cocktail shaker. Pour over the
gin, lychee liqueur and purée,
lemon juice and syrup and
shake well. Strain over ice into
a sling glass. Stir and top up
with soda water. Serve with
long straws and a lychee.

Knockout

4–5 ice cubes
1 measure dry vermouth
½ measure white crème
   de menthe
2 measures gin
1 drop Pernod
lemon slice, to decorate

Put the ice cubes into a mixing
glass. Pour the vermouth, crème
de menthe and gin over the ice,
stir vigorously, then strain into
a chilled old-fashioned glass.
Add the Pernod and serve
with a lemon slice.

Did you know?

Crème de menthe is a sweetish,
mint-flavoured liqueur. It may be
green or white, although the flavour
remains the same. The white
version is used above to blend with
the milky colour of the Pernod.

Moon River

4–5 ice cubes
½ measure dry gin
½ measure apricot brandy
½ measure Cointreau
¼ measure Galliano
¼ measure fresh lemon
   juice
cocktail cherry, to decorate

Put some ice cubes into a
mixing glass. Pour the gin,
apricot brandy, Cointreau,
Galliano and lemon juice over
the ice, stir then strain into a
large chilled cocktail glass.
Decorate with a cherry.

Abbey Road

6 mint leaves
1 piece candied ginger
½ measure fresh lemon
    juice
2 measures gin
1 measure apple juice
ice cubes, plus crushed
    ice to serve
lemon wedge, to decorate

Muddle the mint leaves, ginger
and lemon juice in a cocktail
shaker. Add the gin, apple juice
and some ice cubes and shake
well. Strain over crushed ice in
an old-fashioned glass and
decorate with a lemon wedge.

Collinson

3 ice cubes, cracked
1 dash orange bitters
1 measure gin
½ measure dry vermouth
¼ measure kirsch
lemon rind
½ strawberry and lemon
    slice, to decorate

Put the cracked ice into a
mixing glass, then add the
bitters, gin, vermouth and
kirsch. Stir well and strain
into a cocktail glass. Squeeze
the zest from the lemon
rind over the surface, and
decorate the rim of the glass
with the strawberry half and
lemon slice.

The Fix

2 measures gin
1 dash pineapple syrup
1 dash fresh lime juice
1 dash fresh lemon juice
1 dash Cointreau
6–8 ice cubes
lemon rind and fresh
    pineapple wedges, to
    decorate

Put the gin, pineapple syrup,
fruit juices and Cointreau into
a cocktail shaker and shake well.
Strain into an old-fashioned
glass over the ice cubes and
decorate with the lemon rind
and pineapple wedges.

Night of Passion

6–8 ice cubes
2 measures gin
1 measure Cointreau
1 tablespoon fresh
 lemon juice
2 measures peach nectar
2 tablespoons passion
 fruit juice

Put half the ice cubes with the gin, Cointreau, lemon juice, peach nectar and passion fruit juice into a cocktail shaker and shake well. Strain over the remaining ice into an old-fashioned glass.

Pink Clover Club

4–5 ice cubes
juice of 1 lime
1 dash grenadine
1 egg white
3 measures gin
strawberry slice, to decorate

Put the ice cubes into a cocktail shaker. Pour the lime juice, grenadine, egg white and gin over the ice. Shake until a frost forms, then strain into a cocktail glass. Decorate with a strawberry slice and serve with a straw.

Did you know?

Grenadine is a sweet non-alcoholic syrup made from pomegranates, which give it its attractive, rich rosy-pink colour. It is used in many cocktail creations.

Clover Club

ice cubes
juice of 1 lime
½ teaspoon sugar syrup
1 egg white
3 measures gin
grated lime rind and lime
 wedge, to decorate

Put some ice cubes into a cocktail shaker. Pour the lime juice, sugar syrup, egg white and gin over the ice and shake to mix. Strain over 5–6 ice cubes in an old-fashioned glass. Decorate with grated lime rind and a lime wedge.

Delft Donkey

3–4 ice cubes, cracked
2 measures gin
juice of 1 lemon
ginger beer, to top up
lemon slice, to decorate

Put the cracked ice into a cocktail shaker and pour over the gin and lemon juice. Shake until a frost forms. Pour into a hurricane glass or large tumbler. Top up with ginger beer. Decorate with a lemon slice and serve with a straw.

Gin Cup

3 mint sprigs, plus extra
  to decorate
1 teaspoon sugar syrup
ice cubes, cracked
juice of ½ lemon
3 measures gin

Muddle the mint and sugar syrup in an old-fashioned glass. Fill the glass with cracked ice, add the lemon juice and gin and stir until a frost begins to form. Decorate with extra mint sprigs.

Maiden's Blush

ice cubes
2 measures gin
1 measure Pernod
1 teaspoon grenadine

Put some ice cubes into a cocktail shaker and pour over the gin, Pernod and grenadine. Shake well and strain into a cocktail glass.

Zaza

5–6 ice cubes
3 drops orange bitters
1 measure Dubonnet
2 measures gin

Put the ice cubes into a mixing glass. Shake the bitters over the ice, pour in the Dubonnet and gin and stir vigorously without splashing. Strain into a chilled cocktail glass.

Maiden's Prayer

ice cubes
2 measures gin
2 measures Cointreau
1 measure orange juice

Fill a cocktail shaker three-quarters full with ice cubes. Pour over the gin, Cointreau and orange juice and shake well. Strain into a chilled cocktail glass.

Did you know?
Cointreau is a French liqueur flavoured with oranges. It is clear, unlike Grand Marnier, which has a golden colour.

Gin Garden

¼ cucumber, peeled
    and chopped
½ measure elderflower
    cordial
2 measures gin
1 measure pressed
    apple juice
ice cubes
peeled cucumber slices,
    to decorate

Muddle the chopped cucumber and elderflower cordial in a cocktail shaker. Add the gin, apple juice and some ice cubes and shake well. Double strain into a chilled Martini glass and decorate with cucumber slices.

Gin Garden ▶

By Invitation Only

3 measures gin
2 teaspoons sugar syrup
2 teaspoons fresh lime juice
1 egg white
ice cubes
1 tablespoon crème
   de mure
blackberries, to decorate

Put the gin, sugar syrup, lime juice and egg white into a cocktail shaker and shake to mix. Strain into a highball glass filled with ice cubes and lace with the crème de mure. Decorate with blackberries.

Fair Lady

lightly beaten egg white
   and caster sugar, to frost
ice cubes
1 measure gin
4 measures grapefruit juice
1 dash Cointreau

Frost the rim of an old-fashioned glass by dipping into egg white and pressing into sugar. Put some ice cubes into a cocktail shaker and pour over the remaining egg white, gin, grapefruit juice and Cointreau. Shake well, then pour into the prepared glass.

Turf

ice cubes
1 measure gin
1 measure dry vermouth
1 teaspoon lemon juice
1 teaspoon Pernod
lemon slice, to decorate

Put some ice cubes into a cocktail shaker and pour over gin, vermouth, lemon juice and Pernod. Shake well, then strain into a glass containing more ice. Decorate with a lemon slice.

Did you know?
The connoisseurs' choice of vermouth is Noilly Prat, which was first created by a herbalist, Joseph Noilly, in 1813, using a blend of Blancs de Blancs wines, a little raspberry and lemon and a closely guarded secret mix of herbs and spices. Its flavour is further enhanced by being left to mature in oak casks.

Broadhurst Drive-by

ice cubes
1½ measures gin
1 measure sweet vermouth
1 dash fresh lime juice
1 measure apple juice
green apple slice and
    cocktail cherry,
    to decorate

Put some ice cubes with the gin, vermouth and fruit juices into a cocktail shaker and shake to mix. Strain into a cocktail glass and decorate with a green apple slice and a cherry.

Fighting Bob

ice cubes
2 measures gin
½ measure Chartreuse
½ measure cherry brandy
1 teaspoon lemon juice
1 dash Angostura bitters
soda water, to taste

Put some ice cubes into a cocktail shaker and pour over the gin, Chartreuse, cherry brandy, lemon juice and bitters. Shake well, pour into a highball glass or tumbler and add soda water to taste.

French Kiss

crushed ice
1 measure gin
1 measure Dubonnet
1 measure dry vermouth
1 cocktail cherry, to decorate

Put some crushed ice into a mixing glass, add the gin, Dubonnet and vermouth and stir well. Strain into a glass and decorate with a cherry.

Did you know?
Dubonnet, with its sweet, warm, slightly spicy flavour, is the classic French red wine-based aperitif, invented in Paris in 1846. But there is also a white version – Dubonnet Blanc – made from fortified white wine and herbs.

Bronx

cracked ice, plus ice cubes
    to serve
1 measure gin
1 measure sweet vermouth
1 measure dry vermouth
2 measures orange juice
orange slices, to decorate
cocktail cherry, to decorate

Put some cracked ice into a
cocktail shaker and pour over
the gin, vermouths and orange
juice. Shake to mix. Strain into
an old-fashioned glass over
some ice cubes. Decorate
with orange slices and a
cocktail cherry.

Red Lion

ice cubes
1½ measures Grand
    Marnier
1 tablespoon gin
2 teaspoons orange juice
2 teaspoons lemon juice
lemon rind twist, to
    decorate

Put some ice cubes into a
cocktail shaker and pour over
the Grand Marnier, gin and
fruit juices. Shake well and
strain into a glass over more ice
cubes. Decorate with a lemon
rind twist.

Red Cloud

ice cubes
1½ measures gin
2 teaspoons apricot liqueur
2 teaspoons lemon juice
1 teaspoon grenadine
1–2 dashes Angostura
    bitters

Put some ice cubes into a
cocktail shaker and pour over
the gin, apricot liqueur, lemon
juice, grenadine and bitters.
Shake well, strain into a glass
and add more ice cubes.

Did you know?
Reputedly one of the earliest
liqueurs ever produced, apricot
liqueur is a sweeter, less potent
variation on apricot brandy, with
additional almond undertones. But
apricot brandy can be used in Red
Cloud instead.

Eureka

ice cubes
1 measure gin
½ measure grenadine
½ measure lemon juice
½ measure orange juice
orange slice, to decorate

Put some ice cubes into a cocktail shaker and pour over the gin, grenadine and fruit juices. Shake well and strain into a glass. Decorate with an orange slice.

Mississippi Mule

ice cubes
1½ measures gin
1 teaspoon crème de cassis
1 teaspoon lemon juice

Put some ice cubes into a cocktail shaker and pour over the gin, crème de cassis and juice. Shake well, strain into a glass and add more ice cubes.

Bitter-sweet Symphony

ice cubes
1 measure gin
1 measure Campari
½ measure passion fruit syrup
½ measure fresh lemon juice
lemon slices, to decorate

Put some ice cubes with the gin, Campari, passion fruit syrup and lemon juice into a cocktail shaker and shake to mix. Strain into an old-fashioned glass over 4–6 ice cubes and decorate with lemon slices.

Boxcar

ice cubes
1¼ measures Cointreau
1¼ measures gin
1 teaspoon lime juice
1 egg white
1–2 dashes grenadine
caster sugar

Put some ice cubes into a cocktail shaker and pour over the Cointreau, gin, lime juice, egg white and grenadine. Shake extremely well. Frost the rim of a glass by dipping in water and pressing in sugar. Strain the cocktail into the prepared glass.

North Pole

1 measure gin
½ measure lemon juice
½ measure maraschino
    liqueur
1 egg white
whipping cream,
    to decorate

Put the gin, lemon juice, maraschino and egg white into a cocktail shaker and shake well. Pour into a cocktail glass and decorate with a whipped cream topping.

Negroni

ice cubes
1 measure Plymouth gin
1 measure Campari
1 measure red vermouth
soda water, to top up
    (optional)
orange slices, to decorate

Put some ice cubes with the gin, Campari and vermouth into a cocktail shaker and shake to mix. Strain into an old-fashioned glass filled with ice cubes, top up with soda water, if you like, and decorate with orange slices.

Poet's Dream

4–5 ice cubes
1 measure Bénédictine
1 measure dry vermouth
3 measures gin
lemon rind slice

Put the ice cubes into a mixing glass. Pour the Bénédictine, vermouth and gin over the ice and stir vigorously, without splashing. Strain into a chilled cocktail glass. Twist the lemon rind slice over the drink, then drop it in.

Did you know?
Bénédictine has been made for almost 500 years, originally by the monks of Fécamp Abbey. When mixed with an equal quantity of brandy, it is known as a B&B.

Paradise

3 ice cubes, cracked
1 dash fresh lemon juice
½ measure fresh orange juice
1 measure gin
½ measure apricot brandy
orange and lemon slices, to decorate

Put the cracked ice into a cocktail shaker. Pour over the fruit juices, gin and apricot brandy and shake well. Strain into a chilled cocktail glass and decorate with orange and lemon slices.

Kiss in the Dark

4–5 ice cubes
1 measure gin
1 measure cherry brandy
1 teaspoon dry vermouth

Put the ice cubes into a cocktail shaker. Pour over the gin, cherry brandy and vermouth and shake well. Strain into a chilled cocktail glass.

Bijou

3 ice cubes
1 measure gin
½ measure green
    Chartreuse
½ measure sweet vermouth
1 dash orange bitters
1 green olive and some
    lemon rind, to decorate

Put the ice cubes into a mixing
glass and add the gin,
Chartreuse, vermouth and
bitters. Stir well and strain into
a cocktail glass. Impale the
olive on a cocktail stick and add
to the cocktail, then squeeze the
zest from the lemon rind over
the surface and drop it in.

Monkey Gland

3–4 ice cubes
1 measure orange juice
2 measures gin
3 dashes Pernod
3 dashes grenadine

Put the ice cubes with the
orange juice, gin, Pernod and
grenadine into a cocktail
shaker. Shake well, then strain
into a chilled cocktail glass.

Honolulu

4–5 ice cubes
1 measure pineapple juice
1 measure fresh lemon juice
1 measure fresh orange
    juice
½ teaspoon grenadine
3 measures gin
pineapple slice and cocktail
    cherry, to decorate

Put the ice cubes into a cocktail
shaker and pour over the fruit
juices, grenadine and gin.
Shake until a frost forms. Strain
into a chilled cocktail glass and
decorate with a pineapple slice
and a cherry.

Woodstock

2–3 ice cubes, crushed
1 measure gin
1 measure dry vermouth
¼ measure Cointreau
1 measure fresh orange
    juice
orange rind
orange slice, to decorate

Put the ice into a cocktail shaker and add the gin, vermouth, Cointreau and orange juice. Shake to mix, then strain into a chilled cocktail glass. Squeeze the zest from the orange rind over the surface and decorate with the orange slice twisted over the rim of the glass.

Perfect Lady

ice cubes
2 measures gin
1 measure peach brandy
1 measure lemon juice
1 dash egg white

Fill a mixing glass three-quarters full with ice cubes. Add the gin, peach brandy, lemon juice and egg white and stir well. Strain into a chilled cocktail glass.

Luigi

ice cubes
1 measure fresh orange
    juice
1 measure dry vermouth
½ measure Cointreau
1 measure grenadine
2 measures gin
blood orange slice,
    to decorate

Put some ice cubes into a mixing glass. Pour the orange juice, vermouth, Cointreau, grenadine and gin over the ice and stir vigorously. Strain into a chilled cocktail glass. Decorate with an orange slice.

Ginger Tom

ice cubes
1½ measures gin
1 measure Cointreau
1 dash fresh lime juice
1 dash sweetened ginger
 syrup
1½ measures cranberry
 juice
lime rind spiral, to decorate

Put some ice cubes with the
gin, Cointreau, lime juice,
ginger syrup and cranberry
juice into a cocktail shaker and
shake to mix. Strain into a
chilled cocktail glass and
decorate with a lime rind spiral.

Juliana Blue

crushed ice, plus 2–3 ice
 cubes
1 measure gin
½ measure Cointreau
½ measure blue Curaçao
2 measures pineapple juice
½ measure fresh lime juice
1 measure coconut cream
pineapple slice and cocktail
 cherries, to decorate

Put some crushed ice into a
food processor or blender and
pour in the gin, Cointreau, blue
Curaçao, fruit juices and
coconut cream. Blend at high
speed for several seconds until
the mixture has the consistency
of soft snow. Strain over ice
cubes in a cocktail glass.
Decorate with a pineapple slice
and cherries.

Red Kiss

3 ice cubes, cracked
1 measure dry vermouth
½ measure gin
½ measure cherry brandy
cocktail cherry and lemon
 rind spiral, to decorate

Put the cracked ice into a
mixing glass, add the vermouth,
gin and cherry brandy and stir
well. Strain into a chilled
cocktail glass and decorate
with a cherry and a lemon
rind spiral.

Did you know?
This is a sweeter, fuller-mouthed
twist on French Kiss (see page 95),
using cherry brandy instead of
Dubonnet. Decorate with a green
cocktail cherry for an effective
colour contrast.

Crossbow

drinking chocolate powder
4–5 ice cubes
½ measure gin
½ measure crème de cacao
½ measure Cointreau

Frost the rim of a chilled
cocktail glass by dipping into
a little water and pressing
into drinking chocolate powder.
Put the ice cubes into a cocktail
shaker and add the gin, crème
de cacao and Cointreau. Shake
vigorously and strain into the
prepared glass.

Opera

4–5 ice cubes
1 measure Dubonnet
½ measure Curaçao
2 measures gin
orange rind spiral,
    to decorate

Put the ice cubes into a mixing
glass. Pour the Dubonnet,
Curaçao and gin over the ice.
Stir evenly, then strain into a
chilled cocktail glass. Decorate
with an orange rind spiral.

Park Lane Special

ice cubes
2 measures gin
½ measure apricot brandy
½ measure fresh orange
    juice
1 dash grenadine
½ egg white

Put some ice cubes into a
cocktail shaker and pour over
the remaining ingredients.
Shake well and strain into a
cocktail glass.

Classic Dry Martini

½ measure dry vermouth
3 measures ice-cold gin
green olive or lemon rind
    twist, to decorate

Swirl the vermouth around the inside of a chilled Martini glass, then discard the excess. Pour in the ice-cold gin and add an olive or lemon rind twist.

Did you know?
There are several variations to the Dry Martini. The Dickens is a straightforward drink served without any kind of embellishment. The Gibson is decorated with 2 cocktail onions and the Franklin with 2 green olives, while the Bradford is prepared in a cocktail shaker and shaken rather than stirred.

Gibson Shot

1 dash Noilly Prat
1 measure ice-cold gin
2 pearl onions

Swirl the Noilly Prat around the inside of a chilled shot glass, then discard any excess. Pour in the ice-cold gin. Decorate with the 2 pearl onions, to be eaten after drinking the shot.

The Doobs Martini

ice cubes
2 teaspoons dry vermouth
2 measures gin
1 measure sloe gin
4 dashes orange bitters
orange rind twist, to
    decorate

Put some ice cubes into a cocktail shaker. Add the vermouth and shake well, then strain away the excess. Add the gin, sloe gin and bitters, stir, then strain into a chilled cocktail glass. Decorate with an orange rind twist.

Did you know?
Vermouth is a fortified white wine flavoured with bitter herbs, and comes from France, Italy and the United States. It can be sweet or dry. A red version is also made.

Smoky

ice cubes
¼ measure dry vermouth
2 measures gin
1 measure sloe gin
5 drops of orange bitters
orange rind twist, to
 decorate

Put the ice cubes into a mixing glass, add the vermouth and stir until the ice cubes are well coated. Pour in the gin, sloe gin and bitters and stir well, then strain into a chilled cocktail glass and add an orange rind twist.

Pink Gin

1–4 dashes Angostura
 bitters
1 measure gin
iced water, to top up

Shake the bitters into a cocktail glass and swirl it around to coat the inside. Add the gin, then top up with iced water to taste.

Did you know?

Angostura bitters were developed in the South American town of Angostura in the nineteenth century. Originally intended for medicinal use, they were first put into glasses of gin by the Royal Navy, thus inventing the Pink Gin. Using orange bitters instead of Angostura bitters, transforms the drink into a Yellow Gin.

Gimlet

2 measures gin
1 measure lime cordial
ice cubes
½ measure water
lime wedge, to decorate

Put the gin and lime cordial into a mixing glass, fill up with ice cubes and stir well. Strain into a chilled cocktail glass, add the water, then squeeze the lime wedge into the cocktail before adding it to the drink.

Lady of Leisure

ice cubes
1 measure gin
½ measure Chambord
½ measure Cointreau
1 dash fresh lemon juice
1 measure pineapple juice
orange rind strips, to
    decorate

Put some ice cubes with the gin, Chambord, Cointreau and fruit juices into a cocktail shaker and shake to mix. Strain into a chilled cocktail glass and decorate with orange rind strips.

Stormy Weather

3 ice cubes, cracked
1½ measures gin
¼ Mandarine Napoléon
¼ measure dry vermouth
¼ measure sweet vermouth
orange rind spiral, to
    decorate

Put the cracked ice into a cocktail shaker and add the gin, Mandarine Napoléon and the vermouths. Shake to mix and strain into a chilled cocktail glass. Decorate the rim of the glass with an orange rind spiral.

White Lady

1 measure gin
1 measure Cointreau
1 measure lemon juice
lemon rind twist, to
    decorate (optional)

Pour the gin, Cointreau and lemon juice into a cocktail shaker. Shake well, strain into a chilled Martini glass and decorate with a lemon rind twist if liked.

White Lady ▶

New Orleans Dry Martini

5–6 ice cubes
2–3 drops Pernod
1 measure dry vermouth
4 measures gin

Put the ice cubes into a mixing glass. Pour the Pernod over the ice, then pour in the vermouth and gin. Stir (never shake) vigorously and evenly without splashing. Strain into a chilled cocktail glass.

Vampire

1 measure dry vermouth
1 measure gin
½ measure lime juice

Put all the ingredients into a cocktail shaker and shake well. Pour into a chilled cocktail glass.

Sapphire Martini

4 ice cubes
2 measures gin
½ measure blue Curaçao
red or blue cocktail cherry,
    to decorate

Put the ice cubes into a cocktail shaker. Pour in the gin and blue Curaçao. Shake well to mix. Strain into a cocktail glass and carefully drop in a cherry.

Aviation

ice cubes
2 measures gin
½ measure Maraschino
    liqueur
½ measure lemon juice
cocktail cherry, to decorate

Put some ice cubes with the
gin, Maraschino and lemon
juice into a cocktail shaker.
Shake well. Double strain into a
chilled Martini glass. Decorate
with a cherry.

Opal Martini

ice cubes
2 measures gin
1 measure Cointreau
2 measures fresh
    orange juice
orange rind twist,
    to decorate

Put some ice cubes with the
gin, Cointreau and orange juice
into a cocktail shaker and shake
well. Strain into a chilled
cocktail glass. Drape a long
orange rind twist in the drink
and around the stem of the
glass in a swirl.

Papa's Flight

ice cubes
2 measures gin
2 teaspoons Maraschino
    liqueur
1 measure grapefruit juice
1 dash fresh lime juice
1 dash sugar syrup
orange rind, to decorate

Put some ice cubes with the
gin, Maraschino, fruit juices
and sugar syrup into a cocktail
shaker and shake to mix. Strain
into a chilled cocktail glass and
decorate with orange rind.

Did you know?
This variation on Aviation uses lime
and grapefruit juices instead of
lemon, for a more complex flavour.
Pink grapefruit has a sweeter
flavour than the ordinary variety
and works well with gin.

Sydney Fizz

4–5 ice cubes
1 measure fresh lemon juice
1 measure fresh orange
   juice
½ teaspoon grenadine
3 measures gin
soda water, to top up
orange slice, to decorate

Put the ice cubes into a cocktail shaker. Pour the fruit juices, grenadine and gin over the ice and shake vigorously until a frost forms. Strain into an old-fashioned glass and top up with soda water. Decorate with the orange slice.

French 75

1 measure gin
juice of ½ lemon
1 teaspoon caster sugar
chilled Champagne, to
   top up
lemon twist, to decorate

Put the gin, lemon juice and sugar into a Champagne flute and stir well until the sugar has dissolved. Top up with chilled Champagne and decorate with a lemon rind twist.

Did you know?
An effervescent drink, French 75 was invented during the First World War and named after a large artillery gun used by the French in trench warfare. It was originally made with brandy instead of gin.

French 66

1 white sugar cube
6 dashes orange bitters
1 measure sloe gin
juice of ¼ lemon
chilled Champagne, to
   top up
lemon rind strip, to decorate

Soak the sugar cube in the bitters, then drop it into a Champagne flute. Add the sloe gin and lemon juice and stir. Top up with chilled Champagne and decorate with a lemon rind strip.

Did you know?
Sloe gin is made by flavouring gin with sugar and sloes – hedgerow fruits rather like tiny bitter plums.

Honeydew

3–4 ice cubes, cracked
1 measure gin
½ measure fresh lemon
    juice
1 dash Pernod
50 g (2 oz) honeydew
    melon, diced
Champagne, to top up

Put the cracked ice, gin, lemon
juice, Pernod and melon into a
food processor or blender and
blend for 30 seconds, then pour
into a large wine glass. Top up
with Champagne.

Mbolero

2 lime wedges
2 measures gin
6 mint leaves
6 drops orange bitters
1 dash sugar syrup
ice cubes
mint sprig, to decorate

Squeeze the lime wedges into
a cocktail shaker. Add the gin,
mint leaves, bitters, sugar syrup
and some ice cubes and shake
well. Double strain into a
chilled Martini glass. Decorate
with a mint sprig.

Tipperary

4–5 ice cubes
juice of 1 lemon
3 measures gin
3 measures dry vermouth

Put the ice cubes into a mixing
glass. Pour the lemon juice, gin
and vermouth over the ice. Stir
evenly and strain into a chilled
cocktail glass.

Sloe Gin Sling

1 measure sloe gin
½ measure lemon juice
soda water, to top up
lemon or orange slice,
   to decorate
mint sprig, to decorate

Pour the sloe gin and lemon
juice into a highball glass. Top
up with soda water. Decorate
with a lemon or orange slice
and a mint sprig.

Did you know?
This is a beautifully coloured drink
with a smooth, decadent flavour.

Sloe-ho

2 measures sloe gin
1 measure fresh lemon juice
½ measure sugar syrup
½ measure egg white
ice cubes
soda water, to top up
lemon rind, to decorate

Put the sloe gin, lemon juice,
sugar syrup and egg white into
a cocktail shaker and shake
well. Strain into a highball glass
filled with ice cubes and top up
with soda water. Decorate with
a long lemon rind spiral.

San Francisco

ice cubes
1½ measures sloe gin
¼ measure sweet vermouth
¼ measure dry vermouth
1 dash orange bitters
1 dash Angostura bitters
cocktail cherry, to decorate

Put some ice cubes into a
mixing glass. Add the gin,
vermouths and bitters and stir
well. Pour into a cocktail glass
and decorate with a cherry.

Ruby Fizz

ice cubes
juice of ½ lemon
1 teaspoon granulated
    sugar
1 egg white
2 measures sloe gin
2 dashes raspberry syrup or
    grenadine
soda water, to top up

Put some ice cubes into a
cocktail shaker. Add the lemon
the juice, sugar, egg white, gin
and raspberry syrup or
grenadine. Shake well, strain
into a tall tumbler and top up
with the soda water.

Riviera Fizz

ice cubes
1½ measures sloe gin
½ measure lemon juice
½ measure sugar syrup
Champagne, to top up
lemon rind twist, to
    decorate

Put some ice cubes with the
sloe gin, lemon juice and sugar
syrup into a cocktail shaker and
shake well. Strain into a chilled
Champagne flute. Top up with
Champagne, stir and decorate
with a lemon rind twist.

Little Last

ice cubes
1 lime wedge
½ measure gin
1 dash Chambord
1 dash sugar syrup

Squeeze the lime wedge into
a cocktail shaker. Add the ice
cubes, the gin, Chambord and
sugar syrup. Shake briefly
and strain into a shot glass.

Did you know?
Enjoy your gin in one hit with this
delicious drink that combines
Chambord, a raspberry liqueur, and
lime to give the spirit a lift.

Rum

Like a number of other spirits, rum was first distilled during the seventeenth century, but as a consequence of Caribbean sugar cane production. Rum was developed as a way to use up the by-product of the cane industry, so it was cheap and also relatively quick to produce. It became popular with sailors, and was distributed as part of their daily rations at sea for several centuries. The ships laden with sugar returning to Europe also brought rum and it quickly became popular in England and in other countries with ties to the Caribbean islands.

There are two distinct varieties of rum – light and dark – the difference between them being the amount of ageing. Darker rums are aged for anything up to 12 years in charred oak casks, while white rum is aged in stainless steel tanks. Today rum is used in many cocktails – some of the most well known are the Cuba Libre, Mai Tai and Piña Colada. Zombies contain three types of rum – dark, golden and white.

Kinky Witch

ice cubes
1 measure Havana Club
   3-year-old rum
1 measure Havana Club
   Silver Dry rum
½ measure orange Curaçao
½ measure crème de mure
½ measure orgeat syrup
2 measures orange juice
2 measures grapefruit juice
2 teaspoons over-proof rum
grapefruit wedges, to
   decorate

Put some ice cubes with the
Havana Club rums, Curaçao,
crème de mure, orgeat syrup
and fruit juices into a cocktail
shaker and shake well. Strain
into a highball glass filled with
ice cubes, float the over-proof
rum over the surface and
decorate with grapefruit
wedges.

Monoloco Zombie

ice cubes
1 measure white rum
1 measure Navy rum
½ measure apricot brandy
½ measure orange Curaçao
2 measures orange juice
2 measures pineapple juice
½ measure lime juice
1 dash grenadine
½ measure over-proof rum
pineapple wedges, to
   decorate

Put some ice cubes with all the
other ingredients, except the
over-proof rum, into a cocktail
shaker. Shake well. Strain over
ice cubes in a large hurricane
glass. Top with the over-proof
rum and decorate with
pineapple wedges.

Zombie

ice cubes
1 measure dark rum
1 measure white rum
½ measure golden rum
½ measure apricot brandy
juice of ½ lime
1 teaspoon grenadine
2 measures pineapple juice
½ measure sugar syrup
2 teaspoons over-proof rum
pineapple wedge and leaf
   and sugar, to decorate

Put some ice cubes with the
first 3 rums, apricot brandy,
lime juice, grenadine, pineapple
juice and sugar syrup into a
cocktail shaker and shake well.
Pour into a chilled glass without
straining and float the over-
proof rum on top. Decorate with
a pineapple wedge and leaf,
and sprinkle a pinch of sugar
over the top.

Did you know?
The Zombie is a potent draught
probably invented by Don Beach of
Hollywood's Don the Beachcomber
restaurant, to revive the spirits of a
regular who often described himself
as feeling like the living dead!

Havana Zombie

4–5 ice cubes
juice of 1 lime
5 tablespoons pineapple
    juice
1 teaspoon sugar syrup
1 measure white rum
1 measure golden rum
1 measure dark rum

Put the ice cubes into a mixing glass. Pour the fruit juices, sugar syrup and rums over the ice and stir vigorously. Pour the cocktail without straining into a tall glass.

Zombie Prince

crushed ice
juice of 1 lemon
juice of 1 orange
juice of ½ grapefruit
3 drops Angostura bitters
1 teaspoon soft brown sugar
1 measure white rum
1 measure golden rum
1 measure dark rum
lime and orange slices,
    to decorate

Put the crushed ice into a mixing glass. Pour the fruit juices over the ice and splash in the bitters. Add the sugar and pour in the rums. Stir vigorously, then pour without straining into a Collins glass. Decorate with lime and orange slices.

Did you know?
A Collins glass is perfect for long drinks – the taller, the better. They are always narrow with slightly tapered or perfectly straight sides.

New Orleans Dandy

4–5 ice cubes
1 measure white rum
½ measure peach brandy
1 dash fresh orange juice
1 dash fresh lime juice
Champagne, to top up

Put the ice cubes into a cocktail shaker. Pour the rum, peach brandy and fruit juices over the ice and shake until a frost forms. Strain into a Champagne flute or tall glass and top up with Champagne.

Tiki Treat

crushed ice
½ ripe mango, peeled and
    stoned, plus extra to
    decorate
3 coconut chunks
1 measure coconut cream
2 measures aged rum
dash lemon juice
1 teaspoon caster sugar

Put a small scoop of crushed ice
with all the other ingredients
into a food processor or blender
and blend until smooth. Serve
in a stemmed hurricane glass
with long straws and decorate
with mango slices.

Piña Colada

ice cubes, cracked
1 measure white rum
2 measures coconut milk
2 measures pineapple juice
star fruit slice, to decorate

Put some cracked ice, rum,
coconut milk and pineapple
juice into a cocktail shaker.
Shake lightly to mix. Strain into
a large glass and decorate with
the star fruit slice.

Serenade

6 ice cubes, crushed
1 measure white rum
½ measure Amaretto
    di Saronno
½ measure coconut cream
2 measures pineapple juice
pineapple slice, to decorate

Put half the ice into a food
processor or blender, add the
rum, Amaretto, coconut cream
and pineapple juice and blend
for 20 seconds. Pour into a
tall glass over the remaining
ice cubes. Decorate with a
pineapple slice and serve
with a straw.

Hawaiian Deluxe

ice cubes
1½ measures coconut rum
½ measure Cointreau
½ measure aged rum
1 measure coconut cream
2 measures pineapple juice
1 dash sugar syrup
1 dash lemon juice
1 dash grenadine
pineapple and coconut
    wedges, to decorate

Put some ice cubes with all the other ingredients, except the grenadine, into a cocktail shaker. Shake well. Strain into a large hurricane glass. Drizzle the grenadine on to the drink and decorate with pineapple and coconut wedges. Serve with long straws.

Tropical Dream

3–4 ice cubes
1 measure white rum
1 measure Midori
1 tablespoon coconut cream
3 tablespoons pineapple
    juice
3 tablespoons fresh
    orange juice
½ measure crème de
    banane
½ banana
banana wedge with skin
    on, to decorate

Put the ice cubes with the rum, Midori, coconut cream and fruit juices into a food processor or blender. Blend for about 10 seconds. Add the crème de banane and the banana and blend for a further 10 seconds. Pour into a tall glass, decorate with a banana wedge and serve with a straw.

Lobsters on South Beach

crushed ice
1 measure white rum
1 measure coconut rum
1 measure mango purée
2 measures mandarin juice
    (fresh if possible)
1 measure coconut cream
4 pineapple chunks
pineapple leaf and mango
    slices, to decorate

Put some crushed ice with the rums, mango purée, mandarin juice, coconut cream and pineapple chunks into a food processor or blender and blend until smooth. Serve in a large highball glass and decorate with a pineapple leaf and mango slices.

Did you know?
The mango purée used in this cocktail above is available from good grocery stores or you can make your own by blending half a peeled fresh mango.

Pink Angel

ice cubes
½ measure white rum
¼ measure advocaat
¼ measure cherry brandy
1 egg white
½ measure heavy cream

Put some ice cubes with the rum, advocaat, cherry brandy, egg white and cream into a cocktail shaker and shake well. Strain into a cocktail glass.

Edgemoor

cracked ice
1 measure dark rum
1 measure white rum
1 measure Irish Mist
3 measures fresh
    pineapple juice
1 teaspoon lime cordial
soda water, to top up
lemon and orange slices,
    to decorate

Put some cracked ice with the rums, Irish Mist, pineapple juice and lime cordial into a cocktail shaker and shake lightly. Strain into a tall glass and top up with soda water. Decorate with lemon and orange slices twisted together.

After Dark Crush

crushed ice
2 measures Barbadian rum
½ measure Koko Kanu
    (coconut rum)
½ measure vanilla syrup
1 measure coconut cream
soda water, to top up
cocktail cherries, to
    decorate

Fill a sling glass with crushed ice, then add, one by one, in order, the rums, vanilla syrup and coconut cream. Stir and top up with soda water. Add more ice and decorate with cherries. Serve with long straws.

Mojito

8 mint leaves
$\frac{1}{2}$ lime, cut into wedges
2 teaspoons cane sugar
crushed ice
$2\frac{1}{2}$ measures white rum
soda water, to top up
mint sprigs, to decorate

Muddle the mint leaves, lime
wedges and sugar in a highball
glass. Fill the glass with
crushed ice and add the rum.
Stir and top up with soda water.
Decorate with mint sprigs.

Limon Mojito

1 lime, quartered
2 teaspoons soft brown
    sugar
8 mint leaves
crushed ice
2 measures Bacardi
    Limon rum
soda water, to top up
    (optional)
lemon and lime slices,
    to decorate

Muddle the lime quarters, sugar
and mint in a highball glass. Fill
the glass with crushed ice and
add the rum. Stir and top up
with soda water, if you like.
Decorate with lemon and lime
slices and serve with straws.

Apple-soaked Mojito

8 mint leaves
$\frac{1}{2}$ lime, cut into wedges
2 teaspoons sugar syrup
2 measures golden rum
crushed ice
1 measure apple juice
mint sprig and red apple
    slices, to decorate

Muddle the mint leaves, lime
and sugar syrup in a cocktail
shaker. Add the rum and
shake well. Strain into a
highball glass filled with
crushed ice and top up with
apple juice. Decorate with a
mint sprig and apple slices.

Did you know?
Apple and mint make a really
refreshing combination, and this
mojito (above) is the perfect
summer party drink.

Pineapple Mojito

6 mint leaves
4 pineapple chunks
2 teaspoons soft
    brown sugar
2 measures golden rum
crushed ice
pineapple juice, to top up
pineapple wedge and mint
    sprig, to decorate

Muddle the mint leaves, pineapple chunks and sugar in a cocktail shaker. Add the rum and shake well. Strain into a glass filled with crushed ice, top up with pineapple juice and stir. Decorate with a pineapple wedge and a mint sprig.

Pink Mojito

6 mint leaves
½ lime
2 teaspoons sugar syrup
3 raspberries
crushed ice
1½ measures white rum
½ measure Chambord
cranberry juice, to top up
mint sprig, to decorate

Muddle the mint leaves, lime, sugar syrup and raspberries in a highball glass. Add some crushed ice and the rum and Chambord. Stir well and top up with cranberry juice. Decorate with a mint sprig.

Havana Beach

½ lime
2 measures pineapple juice
1 measure white rum
1 teaspoon sugar
dry ginger ale, to top up
lime slice, to decorate

Cut the lime into 4 pieces and put in a food processor or blender with the pineapple juice, rum and sugar. Blend until smooth. Pour into a hurricane glass or large goblet and top up with dry ginger ale. Decorate with a lime slice.

> **Did you know?**
> A hurricane glass is so-called because it is shaped like a hurricane lamp. It is ideal for serving long drinks.

St James

3–4 ice cubes
juice of ½ lime or lemon
juice of 1 orange
3 drops Angostura bitters
2 measures white or
    golden rum
2 measures tonic water
lime or lemon slice, to
    decorate

Put the ice cubes into a highball glass and pour in the fruit juices. Shake the bitters over the ice cubes, add the rum and tonic water and decorate with a lime or lemon slice. Stir gently.

Bossanova

ice cubes
2 measures white rum
½ measure Galliano
½ measure apricot brandy
4 measures pressed
    apple juice
1 measure lime juice
½ measure sugar syrup
lime wedges, split, to
    decorate

Put some ice cubes with the rum, Galliano, apricot brandy, fruit juices and syrup into a cocktail shaker and shake well. Strain into a highball glass filled with ice cubes. Decorate with split lime wedges and serve with long straws.

Hummingbird

4–5 ice cubes, crushed
1 measure dark rum
1 measure light rum
1 measure Southern
    Comfort
1 measure fresh
    orange juice
cola, to top up
orange slice, to decorate

Put the crushed ice into a cocktail shaker. Pour the rums, Southern Comfort and orange juice over the ice and shake until a frost forms. Strain into a long glass and top up with cola. Decorate with an orange slice and serve with a straw.

Foxy's Millennium Punch

ice cubes
1½ measures white rum
1 measure dark rum
2 measures cranberry juice
2 measures guava juice
½ measure lime juice
pineapple and lime slices,
    to decorate

Put some ice cubes into a large highball glass. Pour the rums and juices over the ice and stir. Decorate with pineapple and lime slices.

Did you know?

Cranberry juice is just made for cocktails, with its vivid colour and vibrant, tart taste. It is believed to have health-promoting properties too, helping to ward off urinary tract infections, and is also high in vitamin C.

My Tie Collection

ice cubes
2 measures golden rum
1 measure apple juice
½ measure fresh lime juice
1 dash orgeat syrup
6 mint leaves
2 teaspoons Wood's
    Navy Rum
cocktail cherry, pineapple
    wedge and lemon slice,
    to decorate

Put some ice cubes with the golden rum, fruit juice, orgeat syrup and mint leaves into a shaker and shake well. Strain over ice cubes into a highball glass, float the Navy Rum on top and decorate with a cherry, pineapple wedge and lemon slice.

Planter's Punch

ice cubes
2 measures Myer's Jamaican
    Planter's Punch rum
4 drops Angostura bitters
½ measure lime juice
2 measures chilled water
1 measure sugar syrup
orange and lime slices,
    to decorate

Put some ice cubes with the rum, bitters, juice, water and syrup into a cocktail shaker. Shake well. Strain into a highball glass filled with ice cubes. Decorate with orange and lime slices.

St Lucia

4–5 ice cubes
1 measure Curaçao
1 measure dry vermouth
juice of ½ orange
1 teaspoon grenadine
2 measures white or
    golden rum
orange rind spiral and
    cocktail cherry, to
    decorate

Put the ice cubes into a cocktail shaker and pour over the Curaçao, vermouth, orange juice, grenadine and rum. Shake until a frost forms, then pour without straining into a highball glass. Decorate with an orange rind spiral and a cherry.

Jolly Roger

5 ice cubes, cracked
1 measure dark rum
1 measure Galliano
½ measure apricot brandy
3 measures orange juice
apricot, orange and lemon
    slices, to decorate

Put half the cracked ice with the rum, Galliano, apricot brandy and orange juice into a cocktail shaker and shake well. Strain over the remaining ice into a tall glass. Decorate with the fruit slices.

Cuba Libre

ice cubes
2 measures golden rum
juice of ½ lime
cola, to top up
lime wedges, to decorate

Fill a highball glass with ice cubes, pour over the rum and lime juice and stir to mix. Top up with cola and decorate with lime wedges.

Cuban Breeze

ice cubes
3 measures cranberry juice
2 measures Havana Club
   3-year-old rum
2 measures grapefruit juice
lime wedges, to decorate

Fill a highball glass with ice cubes and add the cranberry juice. Put some ice cubes into a cocktail shaker, add the rum and grapefruit juice and shake to mix. Strain over the cranberry juice and decorate with lime wedges.

Cooper Cooler

3–4 ice cubes
2 measures golden rum
3 measures dry ginger ale
1 tablespoon fresh lime or
   lemon juice
lime or lemon slice, to
   decorate

Put the ice cubes into a highball glass. Pour over the rum, dry ginger ale and lime or lemon juice and stir. Decorate with lime or lemon slices.

The Papa Doble

crushed ice
3 measures white rum
½ measure Maraschino
   liqueur
1 measure lime juice
1½ measures grapefruit
   juice
grapefruit wedges, to
   decorate

Put a scoop of crushed ice with the rum, Maraschino and fruit juices into a food processor or blender and blend until smooth. Serve in a highball glass with grapefruit wedges. This drink can be sweetened to taste with sugar syrup, although Hemingway never would.

Did you know?

El Floridita is one of Havana's bars made famous by the writer Ernest Hemingway. Although often heaving with tourists, this bar is still one of the best. Rolando Quinones, the manager there, used to mix Hemingway his famed Papa Doble with no sugar and a triple helping of rum. A more user-friendly version would include half a measure of sugar syrup and 2 measures of rum.

The Papa Doble ▸

First the Money

1 lime
1 teaspoon white crème
    de menthe
crushed ice
1 measure dark rum
¾ measure Toussaint coffee
    liqueur
cola, to top up

Cut the lime into wedges and
muddle with the crème de
menthe in a highball glass. Fill
the glass with crushed ice and
add the rum and Toussaint.
Top up with cola.

Egg Nog

ice cubes
1 egg
1 tablespoon sugar syrup
2 measures rum
6 measures milk
grated nutmeg, to decorate

Half-fill a cocktail shaker with
ice cubes. Add the egg, sugar
syrup, rum and milk and shake
well for about 1 minute. Strain
into a tumbler and sprinkle
with a little grated nutmeg.

Florida Skies

cracked ice
1 measure white rum
¼ measure fresh lime juice
½ measure pineapple juice
soda water, to top up
cucumber or lime slices,
    to decorate

Put some cracked ice into a tall
glass. Put the rum and fruit
juices into a cocktail shaker.
Shake lightly. Strain into the
glass and top up with soda
water. Decorate with cucumber
or lime slices.

Mai Tai

ice cubes, and crushed ice
2 measures golden rum
½ measure orange Curaçao
½ measure orgeat syrup
juice of 1 lime
2 teaspoons Wood's
    Navy Rum
lime rind and mint sprig,
    to decorate

Put some ice cubes with the
golden rum, Curaçao, orgeat
syrup and lime juice into a
cocktail shaker and shake well.
Strain over crushed ice into an
old-fashioned glass, float the
Navy rum on top and decorate
with lime rind and a mint sprig.

St Augustine

ice cubes
1½ measures white rum
1 measure grapefruit juice
1 teaspoon Cointreau
caster sugar
lemon rind twist,
    to decorate

Put some ice cubes into a
cocktail shaker and pour over
the rum, grapefruit juice and
Cointreau. Shake well. Frost the
rim of a glass by dipping into
water, then pressing into the
sugar. Strain the drink into the
prepared glass. Add ice cubes
and a lemon rind twist.

Hurricane

ice cubes
1 measure white rum
1 measure gold rum
2 teaspoons passion
    fruit syrup
2 teaspoons lime juice

Put some ice cubes into a
cocktail shaker and pour over
the rums, passion fruit syrup
and lime juice. Shake well.
Strain the drink into a cocktail
glass and add ice cubes.

Did you know?
For an even fruitier, longer version
of Hurricane, add 1 measure each
of orange juice and pineapple juice.

Rum Old-fashioned

3 ice cubes
1 dash Angostura bitters
1 dash lime bitters
1 teaspoon caster sugar
$\frac{1}{2}$ measure water
2 measures white rum
$\frac{1}{2}$ measure dark rum
lime rind twist, to decorate

Stir 1 ice cube with the bitters,
sugar and water in a heavy-
based old-fashioned glass until
the sugar has dissolved. Add
the white rum, stir and add the
remaining ice cubes. Add the
dark rum and stir once again.
Decorate with a lime rind twist.

Rum Refashioned

1 brown sugar cube
4 dashes Angostura bitters
ice cubes
2 measures aged rum
sugar syrup, to taste
lime rind twist, to decorate

Put the sugar cube into an
old-fashioned glass, then
splash in the bitters, add 2 ice
cubes and stir. Add a quarter
of the rum and another 2 ice
cubes and stir. Continue
building, and stirring, with
the rum and ice cubes, adding
sugar syrup to taste. Decorate
with the lime rind twist.

Bolero

ice cubes
1$\frac{1}{2}$ measures white rum
$\frac{3}{4}$ measure apple brandy
several drops sweet
    vermouth
lemon rind twist,
    to decorate

Put some ice into a cocktail
shaker and pour over the rum,
apple brandy and vermouth.
Shake well. Strain into a glass
and add ice cubes. Squeeze a
lemon rind twist over the glass
and drop it in.

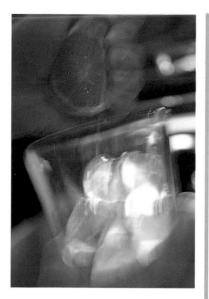

Bahamas Punch

juice of 1 lemon
1 teaspoon sugar syrup
3 drops Angostura bitters
½ teaspoon grenadine
3 measures golden or white
    rum
orange and lemon slices
cracked ice
grated nutmeg, to decorate

Pour the lemon juice and
sugar syrup into a mixing glass.
Shake in the bitters, then add
the grenadine, rum and fruit.
Stir and chill. To serve, fill an
old-fashioned glass with
cracked ice, pour in the punch
without straining and sprinkle
with grated nutmeg.

Chetta's Punch

ice cubes
2 measures Lamb's
    Navy Rum
2 measures undiluted
    blackcurrant cordial
1 tablespoon fresh
    lemon juice
6 dashes orange bitters
orange slices, to decorate

Put some ice cubes with the
rum, blackcurrant cordial,
lemon juice and bitters into
a mixing glass and stir well.
Strain into an old-fashioned
glass filled with ice cubes and
decorate with orange slices.

Did you know?
Named after a Kentish legend
renowned for his alcohol
consumption, the short, sturdy
Chetta's Punch makes the perfect
pick-me-up.

Planter's Cocktail

3 ice cubes, cracked
1 measure dark rum
½ measure fresh orange
    juice
½ measure fresh lemon
    juice
2 dashes Angostura bitters
1 teaspoon icing sugar
pineapple cubes, banana
    slices and orange rind
    spiral, to decorate

Put the cracked ice into a
cocktail shaker and add the
rum, fruit juices, bitters and
sugar. Shake until a frost forms.
Strain into a cocktail glass.
Decorate with the pineapple
cubes, banana slices and an
orange rind spiral.

Pink Treasure

2 ice cubes, cracked
1 measure white rum
1 measure cherry brandy
bitter lemon or soda water,
    to taste (optional)
lemon rind spiral,
    to decorate

Put the cracked ice, rum and
cherry brandy into a glass. Add
a splash of bitter lemon or soda
water, if using. Decorate with a
lemon rind spiral.

White Witch

8–10 ice cubes
1 measure white rum
½ measure white crème
    de cacao
½ measure Cointreau
juice of ½ lime
soda water, to top up
orange and lime slices,
    to decorate

Put half the ice cubes into a
cocktail shaker and pour in the
rum, crème de cacao, Cointreau
and lime juice. Shake and strain
over the remaining ice cubes in
an old-fashioned glass. Top up
with soda water and stir to mix.
Decorate with orange and lime
slices and serve with straws.

Rum Crusta

lime wedge
caster sugar
ice cubes, plus crushed ice
    to serve
2 measures dark rum
1 measure Cointreau
2 teaspoons Maraschino
    liqueur
2 teaspoons fresh lime juice
2 grapes, to decorate

Frost the rim of an old-fashioned
glass by moistening with the
lime wedge and pressing into
the sugar. Put some ice cubes
with the rum, Cointreau,
Maraschino and lime juice into
a cocktail shaker and shake well.
Strain into the old-fashioned
glass filled with crushed ice
and decorate with some grapes.

Beautiful Beth

3–4 ice cubes, crushed
1 measure light rum
1 measure Malibu
½ measure Cointreau
chilled cola, to top up
cocktail cherries, to
    decorate

Put the ice cubes into a cocktail shaker. Pour the rum, Malibu and Cointreau over the ice and shake until a frost forms. Strain into an old-fashioned glass and top up with chilled cola. Decorate with cocktail cherries impaled on a cocktail stick.

Discovery Bay

4–5 ice cubes
3 drops Angostura bitters
juice of ½ lime
1 teaspoon Curaçao or
    blue Curaçao
1 teaspoon sugar syrup
3 measures golden or
    dark rum
lime slices, to decorate

Put the ice cubes into a cocktail shaker, then shake the bitters over the ice. Pour in the lime juice, Curaçao, sugar syrup and rum and shake until a frost forms. Strain into an old-fashioned glass. Decorate with lime slices.

Apricot Daiquiri

crushed ice
1 measure white rum
1 measure fresh lemon juice
½ measure apricot liqueur
    or brandy
3 ripe apricots, skinned
    and stoned
apricot slice, cocktail
    cherry and mint sprig,
    to decorate

Put some crushed ice into a food processor or blender. Add the rum, lemon juice, apricot liqueur or brandy and the apricots and blend for 1 minute or until smooth. Pour into a chilled cocktail glass and decorate with an apricot slice, cocktail cherry and mint sprig.

Strawberry and Mint Daiquiri

3 strawberries, hulled
1 dash strawberry syrup
6 mint leaves, plus extra
    to decorate
ice cubes
2 measures golden rum
2 measures lime juice
strawberry slice, to decorate

Muddle the strawberries, strawberry syrup and mint leaves in a cocktail shaker. Add some ice cubes with the rum and lime juice and shake well. Double strain into a chilled slim Martini glass. Decorate with a strawberry slice and a mint leaf.

Did you know?
There are many variations on the Daiquiri, including frozen fruit Daiquiris and those made with mellow dark rum.

Melon Daiquiri

crushed ice
2 measures rum
2 measures Midori
1 measure lime juice
lime slice, to decorate

Put some crushed ice into a cocktail shaker. Pour the rum, Midori and lime juice over the ice and shake until a frost forms. Strain into a chilled cocktail glass and decorate with a lime slice.

Banana Daiquiri

3 ice cubes, cracked
2 measures white rum
½ measure banana liqueur
½ small banana
½ measure lime cordial
1 teaspoon icing sugar,
    to decorate
banana slice, to decorate

Put the cracked ice into a Margarita glass or tall goblet. Put the rum, banana liqueur, banana and lime cordial into a food processor or blender and blend for 30 seconds. Pour into the glass and decorate with the icing sugar and a banana slice.

Coconut Daiquiri

4–5 crushed ice cubes
2 measures white rum
1 measure coconut liqueur
2 measures fresh lime juice
1 teaspoon grenadine
lime slice, to decorate

Put the crushed ice into a cocktail shaker. Pour the rum, coconut liqueur, lime juice and grenadine over the ice and shake until a frost forms. Strain into a cocktail glass and decorate with a lime slice.

Frozen Mango Daiquiri

crushed ice
½ mango, peeled and stoned
1 measure lime juice
2 measures white rum
1 teaspoon icing sugar
mango slices, to decorate

Put a small scoop of crushed ice into a food processor or blender. Add the mango, lime juice, rum and icing sugar and blend until smooth. Serve in a large glass and decorate with mango slices.

Frozen Mango and Mint Spiced Daiquiri

crushed ice
1 measure fresh lime juice
2 teaspoons sugar syrup
2 measures Morgan Spiced Rum
½ ripe mango, peeled and roughly chopped
6 mint leaves
mango slice and mint sprig, to decorate

Put some crushed ice in a food processor or blender. Add the lime juice, sugar syrup, rum, mango and mint leaves and blend until smooth. Pour into a large Champagne saucer and decorate with a mango slice and a mint sprig.

Frozen Pineapple Daiquiri

crushed ice
2½ pineapple slices
½ measure fresh lime juice
1 measure white rum
¼ measure Cointreau
1 teaspoon sugar syrup
pineapple wedge, to
    decorate

Put some crushed ice into a
food processor or blender.
Add the pineapple slices, lime
juice, rum, Cointreau and sugar
syrup and blend until smooth.
Pour into a chilled cocktail
glass and decorate with a
pineapple wedge.

Port Antonio

½ teaspoon grenadine
4–5 ice cubes
1 measure fresh lime juice
3 measures white or
    golden rum
lime rind and cocktail
    cherry, to decorate

Spoon the grenadine into a
chilled cocktail glass. Put the
ice cubes into a mixing glass.
Pour the lime juice and rum
over the ice and stir vigorously,
then strain into the cocktail
glass. Wrap the lime rind
around the cherry, impale them
on a cocktail stick and use to
decorate the drink.

Bridgetown

4–5 ice cubes
1 measure pineapple juice
3 measures white rum
1 measure dry vermouth
½ teaspoon grenadine

Put the ice cubes in a mixing
glass. Add the pineapple juice,
rum, vermouth and grenadine
and stir vigorously. Pour into a
chilled cocktail glass.

Tobago

½ measure low-proof rum
½ measure gin
1 teaspoon lime juice
1 teaspoon guava syrup
crushed ice

Put the rum, gin, lime juice and guava syrup into a cocktail shaker and shake well. Pour into a glass over crushed ice.

Did you know?
If you roll whole limes around quite hard on a board with your hand, you will find that you get more juice from them.

Black Widow

4–5 ice cubes
2 measures dark rum
1 measure Southern
  Comfort
juice of ½ lime
1 dash sugar syrup
lime slice, to decorate

Put the ice cubes into a cocktail shaker. Pour in the rum, Southern Comfort, lime juice and sugar syrup and shake well. Strain into a chilled cocktail glass and decorate with a lime slice.

Yellow Bird

ice cubes
1½ measures rum
1 measure lime juice
½ measure Galliano
½ measure Triple Sec

Put the ice cubes into a cocktail shaker. Pour in the rum, lime juice, Galliano and Triple Sec and shake well. Strain into a chilled cocktail glass.

Gauguin

3 measures crushed ice
2 measures white rum
2 teaspoons passion
    fruit syrup
2 teaspoons lemon juice
1 teaspoon lime juice
cocktail cherry, to decorate

Put the crushed ice, rum,
passion fruit syrup and fruit
juices into a food processor or
blender and blend at a low
speed for 15 seconds. Strain
into a glass straight up and add
a cherry to decorate.

Bahamas

4–5 ice cubes
1 measure white rum
1 measure Southern
    Comfort
1 measure fresh lemon juice
1 dash crème de banane
lemon slice, to decorate

Put the ice cubes into a cocktail
shaker and pour in the rum,
Southern Comfort, lemon juice
and crème de banane. Shake
vigorously and strain into a
chilled cocktail glass. Add
a thin lemon slice.

Rummy

1 ice cube
½ measure lime juice
¾ measure dry vermouth
½ measure grenadine
1 measure Jamaican rum

Put the ice cube into a cocktail
shaker and pour over the lime
juice, vermouth, grenadine and
rum. Shake well and strain into
a chilled cocktail glass.

Banana Custard

ice cubes
1 measure brandy
1 measure golden rum
½ measure banana liqueur
1 egg
1 measure single cream
½ ripe banana, mashed
3 banana slices, to decorate

Put some ice cubes with the brandy, rum, banana liqueur, egg, cream and banana into a cocktail shaker and shake well. Strain into a goblet and decorate with banana slices.

Did you know?
A comforting concoction based on a popular childhood dessert – but just don't let the kids near this Banana Custard!

El Dorado

4–5 ice cubes
1 measure white rum
1 measure advocaat
1 measure crème de cacao
2 teaspoons grated coconut

Put the ice cubes into a cocktail shaker. Pour the rum, advocaat and crème de cacao over the ice and add the coconut. Shake until a frost forms, then strain into a chilled cocktail glass.

Blue Hawaiian

crushed ice
1 measure white rum
½ measure blue Curaçao
2 measures pineapple juice
1 measure coconut cream
pineapple wedge, to
    decorate

Put some crushed ice into a food processor or blender and pour in the rum, Curaçao, pineapple juice and coconut cream. Blend at high speed for 20–30 seconds. Pour into a chilled cocktail glass. Decorate with a pineapple wedge.

Grenada

4–5 ice cubes
juice of ½ orange
1 measure sweet vermouth
3 measures golden or
    dark rum
ground cinnamon, to
    decorate

Put the ice cubes in a mixing
glass. Pour the orange juice,
vermouth and rum over the ice.
Stir vigorously, then strain into
a chilled cocktail glass. Sprinkle
a little ground cinnamon on top.

Did you know?

The Grenada Cocktail features the
classic flavour combination of rum
and orange, with a slug of sweet
vermouth providing extra
complexity. The cinnamon adds a
lovely spicy warmth – you can use a
sprinkling of ground cinnamon or
pieces of cinnamon stick.

Telford

4–5 ice cubes
1 measure white rum
1 measure dark rum
½ measure tequila
½ measure Cointreau
1 measure apricot brandy
1 measure fresh orange
    juice
2–3 drops orange bitters
1 dash grenadine
cocktail cherries, to
    decorate

Put the ice cubes into a cocktail
shaker. Pour the rums, tequila,
Cointreau, apricot brandy,
orange juice, bitters and
grenadine over the ice and
shake until a frost forms. Strain
into a cocktail glass and
decorate with cherries.

Red Rum

small handful of
    redcurrants
½ measure sloe gin
ice cubes
2 measures Bacardi
    8-year-old rum
½ measure lemon juice
½ measure vanilla syrup
redcurrant string, to
    decorate

Muddle the redcurrants and
sloe gin in a cocktail shaker.
Add the ice cubes with the
remaining ingredients and
shake well. Double strain into
a chilled Martini glass. Decorate
with a redcurrant string.

The Boadas Cocktail

1 measure white rum
1 measure red Dubonnet
1 measure orange Curaçao
cocktail cherries, to
    decorate

Stir the liquid and strain into
a small Martini glass. Decorate
with cherries.

Bacardi Cocktail I

ice cubes
2 measures Bacardi white
    rum
¾ measure fresh lime juice
½ measure grenadine
lime rind, to decorate

Put some ice cubes with the
rum, lime juice and grenadine
into a cocktail shaker and shake
vigorously. Strain into a chilled
cocktail glass and decorate with
lime rind.

Did you know?
In 1936 a New York State Supreme
Court ruled that it is illegal to make
this cocktail without Bacardi rum,
after the Bacardi company tired of
seeing its name used as a generic
term for a rum cocktail.

Bacardi Cocktail II

ice cubes
1½ measures Bacardi
    8-year-old rum
1 measure apple juice
2 teaspoons Chambord
1 teaspoon sugar syrup
2 cocktail cherries, to
    decorate

Put some ice cubes with the
rum, apple juice, Chambord and
sugar syrup into a mixing glass
and stir until chilled. Strain into
a chilled cocktail glass and
decorate with cherries.

Mafia Martini

ice cubes
2 measures golden rum
½ measure Chambord
1 measure apple juice
lime rind twist, to decorate

Put some ice cubes with the
rum, Chambord and apple juice
into a cocktail shaker and shake
briefly. Double strain into a
chilled Martini glass. Decorate
with a lime rind twist.

Almond Cigar

2 measures Havana
  3-year-old rum
1 measure lime cordial
1 measure Amaretto di
  Saronno
cinnamon stick and lime
  rind twist, to decorate

Pour the rum, lime cordial and
Amaretto into a chilled cocktail
shaker. Shake and strain into a
chilled Martini glass. Decorate
with a cinnamon stick and a
lime rind twist.

Did you know?
The stylish Almond Cigar came
second in Havana Rum's worldwide
cocktail contest.

Batiste

4–5 ice cubes
1 measure Grand Marnier
2 measures golden or
  dark rum

Put the ice cubes into a mixing
glass. Pour the Grand Marnier
and rum over the ice, stir
vigorously, then strain into
a cocktail glass.

Passion for Fashion

ice cubes
1½ measures golden rum
½ measure Grand Marnier
2 dashes Angostura bitters
pulp of 1 passion fruit
2 teaspoons passion
    fruit syrup
1 dash lime juice
cocktail cherries, to
    decorate

Put some ice cubes with the
rum, Grand Marnier, bitters,
passion fruit pulp and syrup
and lime juice into a cocktail
shaker. Shake well. Double
strain into a chilled Martini
glass. Decorate with cherries.

Berlin Blonde

ice cubes
1 measure dark rum
1 measure Cointreau
1 measure double cream
ground cinnamon, to
    decorate
cocktail cherry, to decorate

Put some ice cubes with the
rum, Cointreau and cream into
a cocktail shaker and shake
well. Double strain into a
chilled Martini glass. Decorate
with a sprinkle of ground
cinnamon and a cherry.

Havana Club

ice cubes
1½ measures white rum
1 tablespoon dry vermouth

Put some ice cubes with all the
other ingredients into a cocktail
shaker and shake well. Pour
into a chilled Martini glass.

Rude Jude

ice cubes
1 measure white rum
1 dash strawberry purée
1 dash strawberry syrup
1 dash fresh lime juice

Put some ice cubes into a cocktail shaker and pour over the rum, strawberry purée and syrup and lime juice. Shake well and strain into a shot glass.

Spiced Berry

ice cubes
1 measure Morgan
   Spiced Rum
1 dash fresh lime juice
1 dash raspberry purée
1 dash sugar syrup

Put some ice cubes into a cocktail shaker and pour over the rum, lime juice, raspberry purée and sugar syrup. Shake briefly and strain into a chilled shot glass.

Did you know?
Warming spiced rum is given a fruity burst with lime and raspberry in this Spiced Berry, which is the shot equivalent of a hot toddy.

Clem the Cuban

1 dash apple schnapps
1 mint sprig
2 lime wedges
1 measure Havana Club
   3-year-old rum
crushed ice

Muddle the schnapps, mint sprig and lime wedges in a cocktail shaker, then add the rum and a scoop of crushed ice. Shake very briefly and double strain into a shot glass.

Clem the Cuban ▶

Brandy

Arab alchemists first distilled brandy in the seventh and eighth centuries when they occupied Mediterranean states where grapes were grown in profusion. However, the widespread consumption of brandy had to wait until the sixteenth century when space aboard European cargo ships was at a premium. Wine merchants discovered that if the water was removed from wine, more could be packed on board ship. Converts to the scheme soon realized that this concentrate tasted just as good as wine and techniques were developed to produce brandy in its own right.

There are three distinct kinds of brandy: grape brandy, distilled from grape juice and crushed but not pressed grape pulp and skins; Pomace brandy, distilled from pulp, skins and stems; and fruit brandy, distilled from fruits other than grapes. Brandy is graded according to how long it is aged; this can range from two to over eight years.

Parisien

crushed ice
1 measure brandy
½ measure Calvados
1 measure fresh lemon juice
sugar syrup, to taste
½ measure Poire William
apple and pear slices, to
    decorate

Fill a tumbler with crushed ice.
Add the brandy, Calvados,
lemon juice and sugar syrup to
taste. Pour the Poire William
over the top and decorate with
apple and pear slices.

Leo

2–3 ice cubes, crushed
1 measure brandy
1 ½ measures fresh
    orange juice
½ measure Amaretto
    di Saronno
soda water, to taste
1 teaspoon Campari

Put the crushed ice into a
cocktail shaker. Add the brandy,
orange juice and Amaretto and
shake well. Strain into a tall
glass and add soda water to
taste and the Campari.

Did you know?

Campari is an Italian aperitif wine
with a strong, bitter taste and bright
red colour. Amaretto is a liqueur
made from almonds and apricots,
first made in Saronno, Italy, in the
sixteenth century.

Scorpion

5 ice cubes, crushed
1 measure brandy
½ measure white rum
½ measure dark rum
2 measures fresh
    orange juice
2 teaspoons Amaretto
    di Saronno
2–3 dashes Angostura
    bitters
orange or lemon slices,
    to decorate

Put half the crushed ice into
a cocktail shaker and add the
brandy, rums, orange juice,
Amaretto and bitters. Shake
until a frost forms. Strain
over the remaining ice in a tall
glass or goblet. Decorate with
orange or lemon slices and
serve with a straw.

Brandy Sour

4–5 ice cubes
3 drops Angostura bitters
juice of ½ lemon
3 measures brandy
1 teaspoon sugar syrup
lemon slices, to decorate

Put the ice cubes into a cocktail shaker. Shake the bitters over the ice, add the lemon juice, brandy and sugar syrup and shake until a frost forms. Strain over the remaining ice in a glass and decorate with lemon slices impaled on a cocktail stick. Serve with a straw.

Bedtime Bouncer

2 measures brandy
1 measure Cointreau
5 measures bitter lemon
4–6 ice cubes
lemon rind spiral, to decorate

Pour the brandy, Cointreau and bitter lemon into a tumbler, stir well and add the ice. Decorate with a lemon rind spiral and serve with a straw.

Bouncing Bomb

4–5 ice cubes
2 measures brandy
1 measure Curaçao
soda water, to top up
orange rind strip, to decorate

Put the ice cubes into a mixing glass. Pour the brandy and Curaçao over the ice and stir vigorously. Strain into a highball glass and top up with soda water. Decorate with an orange rind strip.

Penguin

1 measure brandy
½ measure Cointreau
1 measure fresh lemon juice
1 measure fresh orange
    juice
1 dash grenadine
ice cubes
¼ orange slice, to decorate
¼ lemon slice, to decorate

Pour the brandy, Cointreau,
fruit juices and grenadine into a
mixing glass and stir well. Pour
into a tall glass filled with ice
cubes. Decorate with the orange
and lemon slice quarters placed
on the rim of the glass. Serve
with 2 long straws.

Monte Carlo Sling

5 seedless grapes, plus
    extra to decorate
crushed ice
1 measure brandy
½ measure peach liqueur
1 measure ruby port
1 measure lemon juice
½ measure orange juice
1 dash orange bitters
2 measures Champagne
grapes, to decorate

Muddle the 5 grapes in a tall
glass, then fill the glass with
crushed ice. Put all the other
ingredients, except the
Champagne, into a cocktail
shaker and add more ice. Shake
well and strain into the glass.
Top up with Champagne and
decorate the glass with grapes.

Macauley

cracked ice
1 measure Cognac
1 measure dry vermouth
2 measures Curaçao
orange rind strip, to
    decorate

Put some cracked ice with the
Cognac, vermouth and Curaçao
into a cocktail shaker. Shake
well. Strain into a tall glass.
Drop the orange rind strip into
the glass.

Sangria

ice cubes
2 bottles light Spanish red
    wine, chilled
4 measures brandy
    (optional)
450 ml (¾ pint) soda
    water, chilled
fruit in season, such as
    apples, pears, lemons,
    peaches and
    strawberries, sliced
orange slices, to decorate

Put some ice cubes into a large
bowl and pour over the wine
and brandy, if using. Stir. Add
the soda water and float the
fruit on top. Serve in tall glasses
and decorate with orange slices.
Serves 10–12

Did you know?

The word 'sangria' comes from
'sangre', the Spanish for blood, and
relates to its deep red colour. Minus
the brandy, and with the option of
adding more soda water and/or
orange or lemon juice, sangria can
make a light, thirst-quenching
drink, perfect for a summer's day.

Fish House Punch

ice cubes
1 measure brandy
1 measure peach brandy
1 measure golden rum
1 measure lemon juice
1 measure cold tea (English
    Breakfast)
½ measure sugar syrup
soda water, to top up
lemon slice, to decorate

Put some ice cubes with the
brandies, rum, lemon juice, tea
and sugar syrup into a cocktail
shaker. Shake well. Double
strain into a highball glass filled
with ice cubes. Top up with soda
water, decorate with a lemon
slice and serve with straws.

Haiti Punch

2 pineapples, peeled and
    cubed
3 lemons, sliced
3 oranges, sliced
300 ml (½ pint) brandy
300 ml (½ pint) Orange
    Nassau liqueur
2 bottles sparkling dry
    white wine

Put the prepared fruit into a
large bowl or jug and pour over
the brandy and Orange Nassau.
Cover and chill for several
hours. To serve, pour about
1 measure of the brandy
mixture into a Champagne
flute, top up with sparkling
wine and add some of the
pineapple cubes.
Serves 12–15

Tidal Wave

6 ice cubes
1 measure Mandarine
    Napoléon
4 measures bitter lemon
1 dash lemon juice
lemon slice, to decorate

Put the ice cubes into a highball
glass. Add the Mandarine
Napoléon, bitter lemon and
lemon juice and stir well.
Decorate with a lemon slice.

Brandy Cuban

2–3 ice cubes
1½ measures brandy
juice of ½ lime
cola, to top up
lime slice, to decorate

Put the ice cubes into a tumbler
and pour over the brandy
and lime juice. Stir vigorously
to mix. Top up with cola and
decorate with a lime slice.
Serve with a straw.

Harlequin

lightly beaten egg white
caster sugar
1 measure kirsch
1 measure apricot brandy
2 measures orange juice
soda water
orange slice and 2 cocktail
    cherries, to decorate

Frost the rim of a tumbler by
dipping into the egg white, then
then pressing into caster sugar.
Put the kirsch, apricot brandy
and orange juice into a cocktail
shaker. Shake lightly. Strain
into the prepared glass and
top up with soda water.
Decorate with an orange slice
and cherries.

Did you know?

The clear, colourless nature of
kirsch, also called cherry schnapps,
belies its powerful, bitter flavour,
derived from black cherries and the
kernels of their stones.

Spiced Sidecar

ice cubes
juice of ½ lemon
2 measures Morgan
    Spiced Rum
1 measure brandy
1 measure Cointreau
lemon and orange rind
    twists, to decorate

Put some ice cubes with the
lemon juice, rum, brandy and
Cointreau into a cocktail shaker
and shake well. Strain into an
old-fashioned glass filled with
ice cubes and decorate with
lemon and orange rind twists.

Brandy Fix

1 teaspoon icing sugar
1 teaspoon water
1 measure brandy
½ measure cherry brandy
juice of ½ lemon
crushed ice
lemon slice, to decorate

Dissolve the sugar in the water
in a mixing glass, then add the
brandy, cherry brandy and
lemon juice. Stir to mix. Pour
into a brandy balloon or small
tumbler. Fill the glass with
crushed ice, float a lemon slice
on top and serve with a straw.

Toulon

4–5 ice cubes
1 measure dry vermouth
1 measure Bénédictine
3 measures brandy
orange rind strip,
    to decorate

Put the ice cubes into a mixing
glass. Pour the vermouth,
Bénédictine and brandy over
the ice and stir vigorously.
Strain into a chilled cocktail
glass and decorate with the
orange rind strip.

Caen-Caen

4–5 ice cubes
2 measures brandy
1 measure Calvados
½ measure sweet vermouth

Put the ice cubes into a mixing glass. Pour the brandy, Calvados and vermouth over the ice and stir vigorously. Strain into a chilled cocktail glass.

Avondale Habit

3 strawberries, hulled
1 dash sugar syrup
4 mint leaves
crushed ice
1½ measures brandy
freshly cracked black
    pepper
2 teaspoons crème
    de menthe
mint sprig and strawberry
    half, to decorate

Muddle the strawberries, sugar syrup and mint leaves in an old-fashioned glass. Almost fill the glass with crushed ice, then add the brandy and cracked pepper. Stir and add more crushed ice, then add the crème de menthe. Decorate with a mint sprig and a strawberry half.

Did you know?
This intriguing mix of flavours – strawberry, mint and black pepper – is unusual but complementary, bringing out the herbal quality of the brandy that is so often ignored.

Shanghai

3 ice cubes, crushed
1 measure brandy
½ measure Curaçao
¼ measure Maraschino
    liqueur
2 dashes Angostura bitters
lemon rind spiral and
    cocktail cherry, to
    decorate

Put the crushed ice into a cocktail shaker. Add the brandy, Curaçao, Maraschino and bitters and shake to mix. Pour into a cocktail glass and decorate with a lemon rind spiral and a cherry impaled on a cocktail stick.

Shanghai ▶

Brandy Manhattan

ice cubes
1 measure sweet vermouth
3 measures brandy
cocktail cherry, to decorate

Put the ice cubes into a mixing glass. Pour the vermouth and brandy over the ice and stir vigorously. Pour into a chilled cocktail glass and decorate with a cherry.

Brandied Boat

crushed ice
1 measure brandy
2 teaspoons lemon juice
1 teaspoon Maraschino bitters
1 measure port
lemon rind spiral, to decorate

Put the crushed ice into a cocktail shaker. Add the brandy, lemon juice and bitters and shake to mix. Pour into a tumbler and pour over the port. Decorate with a lemon rind spiral on the side.

Corpse Reviver

3 ice cubes, cracked
2 measures brandy
1 measure Calvados
1 measure sweet vermouth
apple slice, to decorate

Put the cracked ice into a cocktail shaker. Add the brandy, Calvados and vermouth and shake until a frost forms. Strain into a glass and decorate with an apple slice.

Apricot Sour

2 ice cubes, cracked
1 measure apricot brandy
1 measure lemon juice
1 dash Angostura bitters
1 dash egg white
1 apricot wedge, chopped
lemon slice and cocktail
    cherry, to decorate

Put all the ingredients into
a cocktail shaker and shake
vigorously. Strain into a tumbler
and decorate with a lemon slice
and a cherry impaled on a
cocktail stick.

Fifth Avenue

1 measure brown crème
    de cacao
1 measure apricot brandy
1 measure cream

Pour the crème de cacao into
a straight-sided liqueur glass.
Using the back of a bar spoon,
slowly float the apricot brandy
over the crème de cacao. Pour
the cream over the apricot
brandy in the same way.

Apple Posset

8 measures unsweetened
    apple juice
1 teaspoon soft brown sugar
2 tablespoons Calvados
cinnamon stick

Heat the apple juice in a small
saucepan to just below boiling
point. Meanwhile, measure
the sugar and Calvados into a
warmed mug or glass. Pour the
hot apple juice on to the sugar
and Calvados, stirring with the
cinnamon stick until the sugar
has dissolved.

Monta Rosa

4–5 ice cubes
juice of ½ lime
1 measure Cointreau
3 measures brandy

Put the ice cubes into a mixing
glass. Pour the lime juice,
Cointreau and brandy over the
ice and stir vigorously. Strain
into a chilled cocktail glass.

East India

ice cubes
3 drops Angostura bitters
½ measure pineapple juice
½ measure blue Curaçao
2 measures brandy
orange rind spiral, to
    decorate

Put the ice cubes into a mixing
glass. Shake the bitters over the
ice and pour over the pineapple
juice, Curaçao and brandy. Stir
until frothy, then strain into a
chilled cocktail glass. Decorate
with an orange rind spiral tied
into a knot.

Depth Bomb

4–5 ice cubes
juice of 1 lemon
½ teaspoon grenadine
1 measure Calvados
2 measures brandy
red or green apple slices,
    to decorate

Put the ice cubes into a mixing
glass. Pour the lemon juice,
grenadine, Calvados and
brandy over the ice and stir
vigorously. Strain into a chilled
cocktail glass and decorate with
apple slices.

Stinger

4 ice cubes, cracked
½ measure white crème
   de menthe
1½ measures brandy
mint sprig, to decorate

Put the cracked ice into a
cocktail shaker and pour over
the crème de menthe and
brandy. Shake well. Strain into
a cocktail glass and decorate
with a mint sprig.

Between the Sheets

4–5 ice cubes
1¼ measures brandy
1 measure white rum
½ measure Cointreau
¾ measure fresh lemon
   juice
½ measure sugar syrup

Put the ice cubes into a cocktail
shaker. Add the brandy, rum,
Cointreau, lemon juice and
sugar syrup and shake until a
frost forms. Strain into a chilled
cocktail glass.

From the Rafters

ice cubes
1 measure brandy
1 tablespoon Frangelico
   hazelnut liqueur
1 measure Cointreau
1 measure pineapple juice
cherry slices, to decorate

Put some ice cubes with the
brandy, Frangelico, Cointreau
and pineapple juice into a
cocktail shaker and shake to
mix. Strain into a chilled
cocktail glass and decorate with
cherry slices, which will sink
to the bottom of the glass.

Did you know?
Hazelnut liqueur brings a nutty note
to the From the Rafters, and the
cherry slices at the bottom of the
glass provide an end-of-drink treat,
having soaked up all the wonderful
alcoholic flavours.

Big City Dog

2 dashes Peychaud's bitters
ice cubes
1 measure brandy
½ measure green
 Chartreuse
½ measure cherry brandy

Put the bitters into a brandy balloon and swirl to coat the inside. Turn the glass upside down and let it drain. Put some ice cubes with the brandy, green Chartreuse and cherry brandy into a mixing glass and stir well. Double strain into the brandy balloon.

Did you know?
A brandy balloon allows the drinker to swirl the brandy around inside, warming it against their cupped hands to release the aromas.

Metropolitan

ice cubes, cracked
1 measure brandy
1 measure sweet vermouth
½ teaspoon sugar syrup
3–4 dashes Angostura
 bitters

Put some cracked ice with the brandy, vermouth, sugar syrup and bitters into a cocktail shaker and shake well. Strain into a chilled cocktail glass.

Hop Frog

ice cubes
1 measure brandy
2 measures lime juice

Put some ice cubes with the other ingredients into a cocktail shaker and shake well. Strain into a chilled cocktail glass.

Brandy Crusta

lemon wedge
caster sugar
ice cubes
2 measures brandy
½ measure orange Curaçao
½ measure Maraschino
   liqueur
1 measure fresh lemon juice
3 dashes Angostura bitters
lemon rind, to decorate

Frost the rim of a chilled
cocktail glass by moistening
with the lemon wedge then
pressing in the sugar. Put some
ice cubes with the brandy,
Curaçao, Maraschino, lemon
juice and bitters into a cocktail
shaker and shake well. Strain
into the prepared glass and
decorate with lemon rind.

Applejack Sour

ice cubes
2 measures apple brandy
½ measure lemon juice
1½ teaspoons sugar syrup

Put some ice cubes into a
cocktail shaker and pour over
the apple brandy, lemon juice
and sugar syrup. Shake well.
Strain into a sour glass and
serve straight up or in an old-
fashioned glass over ice.

Brandy Alexander

3 ice cubes, cracked
1 measure brandy
1 measure brown crème
   de cacao
1 measure single cream
cocoa powder, to decorate

Put the cracked ice with the
brandy, crème de cacao and
cream into a cocktail shaker
and shake well. Strain into
a chilled cocktail glass and
sprinkle with cocoa powder.

Did you know?

A Brandy Alexander is a sweet
and creamy after-dinner cocktail
with a chocolate aftertaste. It was
originally made with gin instead of
brandy and called an Alexander.
Use ice cream instead of cream,
blend well and you have a Frozen
Alexander.

Nice Pear

ice cubes
2 measures brandy
1 measure Poire William
1 measure sweet vermouth
peeled pear slices, to
    decorate

Put some ice cubes with the
brandy, Poire William and
vermouth into a cocktail shaker
and shake well. Strain into
a chilled cocktail glass and
decorate with the pear slices.

Brandy Sidecar

4–5 ice cubes
juice of 1 lemon
1 measure Cointreau
2 measures brandy
orange rind spiral
    and cocktail cherry,
    to decorate

Put the ice cubes into a mixing
glass. Pour the lemon juice,
Cointreau and brandy over the
ice and stir vigorously. Strain
into a chilled cocktail glass.
Decorate with an orange rind
spiral and a cherry impaled
on a cocktail stick.

Melbourne

4–5 ice cubes
1 measure Curaçao
3 measures brandy
lemon rind, to decorate

Put the ice cubes into a
measuring glass, pour over the
Curaçao and brandy and stir
vigorously. Strain into a chilled
cocktail glass. Squeeze the zest
from the lemon rind over the
drink, then drop it in.

Banana Bliss

4–5 ice cubes
1 measure brandy
1 measure crème de banane
1 measure Cointreau
lemon juice
banana slice, to decorate

Put the ice cubes into a mixing glass and pour over the brandy, crème de banane and Cointreau. Stir with a spoon, then strain into a cocktail glass. Dip the banana slice in lemon juice to prevent it discolouring. Attach to the rim of the glass.

Brandy Classic

4–5 ice cubes, plus cracked ice to serve
1 measure brandy
1 measure blue Curaçao
1 measure Maraschino liqueur
juice of ½ lemon
lemon wedge, to decorate

Put the ice cubes into a cocktail shaker. Pour in the brandy, Curaçao, Maraschino and lemon juice and shake to mix. Strain into a chilled cocktail glass. Add some cracked ice and a lemon wedge.

Did you know?
Blue Curaçao is a dazzling blue, orange-flavoured liqueur, made with the dried peel of the green oranges that come from the Caribbean island of the same name. It is also available in several other colours.

American Beauty

4–5 ice cubes
1 measure brandy
1 measure dry vermouth
1 measure orange juice
1 measure grenadine
1 dash crème de menthe
2–3 dashes ruby port
cocktail cherry and orange slice, to decorate
mint sprig, to decorate

Put the ice cubes into a cocktail shaker. Pour in the brandy, vermouth, orange juice, grenadine and crème de menthe and shake well. Strain into a cocktail glass. Tilt the glass and gently pour in a little ruby port so that it floats on top. Decorate with a cherry, an orange slice and a mint sprig impaled on a cocktail stick.

American Rose

4–5 ice cubes, plus crushed
    ice to serve
1 measure brandy
1 dash Pernod
1 dash grenadine
½ ripe peach, skinned,
    stoned and roughly
    chopped
Champagne, to top up
peach or mango slices,
    to decorate

Put the ice cubes into a cocktail
shaker. Pour in the brandy,
Pernod and grenadine and add
the peach. Shake well, then
strain into a cocktail glass filled
with crushed ice. Top up with
Champagne just before serving
and add peach or mango slices
to decorate.

Morning

4–5 ice cubes
3 dashes Angostura bitters
5 dashes Pernod
½ teaspoon grenadine
½ teaspoon dry vermouth
1 measure Curaçao
3 measures brandy
cocktail cherries, to
    decorate

Put the ice cubes into a cocktail
shaker. Shake the bitters over
the ice and add the Pernod.
Pour in the grenadine,
vermouth, Curaçao and brandy,
shake well, then strain into a
chilled cocktail glass. Decorate
with cherries impaled on a
cocktail stick.

Christmas Punch

juice of 15 lemons
juice of 4 oranges
625 g (1¼ lb) sugar
ice cubes
300 ml (½ pint) orange
    Curaçao
2 measures grenadine
2 measures brandy
2.5 litres (4 pints) sparkling
    mineral water
orange and lemon rind,
    to decorate

Pour the fruit juices into a jug.
Add the sugar and stir gently
until it has dissolved. Put a
large quantity of ice cubes into
a large punch bowl. Add the
fruit juices, Curaçao, grenadine,
brandy and mineral water and
stir well. Decorate with the
orange and lemon rind before
serving.
Serves 15–20

Angel Face

3 ice cubes, cracked
1 measure gin
1 measure apricot brandy
1 measure Calvados
orange rind twist, to
    decorate

Put the cracked ice into a
cocktail shaker and pour over
the gin, apricot brandy and
Calvados. Shake well. Strain
into a cocktail glass and add an
orange rind twist.

Jaffa

3 ice cubes, cracked
1 measure Mandarine
    Napoléon brandy
1 measure brown crème
    de cacao
1 measure single cream
cocoa powder, to decorate

Put the cracked ice with the
brandy, crème de cacao and
cream into a cocktail shaker
and shake well. Strain into a
chilled cocktail glass and
sprinkle with cocoa powder.

Did you know?
Mandarine Napoléon is a brandy
flavoured with mandarin oranges.
With the addition of orange bitters,
Jaffa is a great combination of
chocolate and orange.

Burnt Orange

4–5 ice cubes
3 drops orange bitters or
    Angostura bitters
juice of ½ orange
3 measures brandy
orange slice, to decorate

Put the ice cubes into a cocktail
shaker. Shake the bitters over
the ice, add the orange juice
and brandy and shake
vigorously. Strain into a chilled
cocktail glass and decorate with
an orange slice.

Brandy Flip

ice cubes
1 egg
2 measures brandy
1½ teaspoons caster sugar
grated nutmeg, to decorate

Put some ice cubes with the egg, brandy and sugar into a cocktail shaker and shake well. Strain into a brandy balloon and sprinkle a little grated nutmeg on top.

Did you know?

A flip is a spirit or wine shaken with egg and sugar until frothy, then dusted with nutmeg. The version here features brandy, but port, rum, sherry or whisky can be used. Early flips were warmed by plunging a red-hot poker, called a 'flip-iron', into the drink just before serving.

The Pudding Cocktail

1 measure Calvados
1½ measures brandy
1 egg yolk
1 teaspoon caster sugar
ice cubes
ground cinnamon, to decorate

Put the Calvados, brandy, egg yolk and caster sugar into a shaker with some ice cubes and shake until well mixed. Strain into a chilled cocktail glass. Light a long taper, hold it over the glass and sprinkle cinnamon through the flame on to the surface of the drink.

Angel's Kiss

½ measure crème de cacao
½ measure brandy
½ measure lightly whipped double cream

Pour the crème de cacao into a shot glass. Using the back of a bar spoon, slowly float the brandy over the crème de cacao. Pour the cream over the brandy in the same way.

Angel's Kiss ▶

Tequila

This fiery drink originated in Mexico at the time of the Aztecs and was drunk by the Spanish conquistadors before its popularity spread to America. Contrary to popular belief, tequila is actually made from the blue agave plant and not the cactus. Although it is often blended with sugar, to pass officially as tequila, the drink must contain no less that fifty-one per cent blue agave. There are some brands that are one hundred per cent blue agave, but these must be rigorously checked to ensure authenticity. Although tequila has traditionally been drunk as a 'slammer' with salt and lime, it has attracted a more discerning drinker over the years and the best tequilas should be sipped like a good brandy or whisky. However, the most common way to drink tequila is in the famous Margarita cocktail.

Playa Del Mar

ice cubes
1 orange slice
light brown sugar and sea
    salt, mixed
1¼ measures tequila gold
¾ measure Grand Marnier
2 teaspoons fresh lime juice
¾ measure cranberry juice
¾ measure pineapple juice
pineapple wedge and
    orange rind spiral, to
    decorate

Frost the rim of a sling glass
by moistening with the orange
slice, then pressing into the
sugar and salt mixture. Fill the
glass with ice cubes. Pour the
tequila, Grand Marnier and
fruit juices into a cocktail
shaker. Fill the shaker with ice
cubes and shake vigorously for
10 seconds, then strain into the
sling glass. Decorate with a
pineapple wedge and orange
rind spiral.

Matador

crushed ice
1¼ measures tequila
¾ measure fresh lime juice
3 measures pineapple juice
1 pineapple chunk
2 teaspoons sugar syrup
pineapple wedge and lime
    rind spiral, to decorate

Put a handful of crushed ice
with the tequila, fruit juices,
pineapple chunk and sugar
syrup into a food processor
or blender and blend for
15 seconds. Pour into a highball
glass and decorate with a
pineapple wedge and a lime
rind spiral.

Rosarita Bay Breeze

ice cubes
1¼ measures tequila
6 measures cranberry juice
1½ measures pineapple
    juice
orange slice, to decorate

Put some ice cubes into a large
highball glass and pour in the
tequila and cranberry juice.
Float the pineapple juice over
the top of the drink and
decorate with an orange slice.

Sunburn

ice cubes
¾ measure tequila gold
1 tablespoon Cointreau
6 measures cranberry juice
orange slice, to decorate

Fill a large highball glass
with ice cubes and pour in
the tequila, Cointreau and
cranberry juice. Decorate
with an orange slice.

El Diablo

ice cubes
1¼ measures tequila gold
¾ measure lime juice
2 teaspoons grenadine
3½ measures dry ginger ale
lime slice, to decorate

Fill a large highball glass
with ice cubes and pour in
the tequila, lime juice and
grenadine. Top up with dry
ginger ale and stir gently.
Decorate with a lime slice.

Texas Tea

ice cubes
¾ measure tequila
1 tablespoon white rum
1 tablespoon Cointreau
2 teaspoons sugar syrup
¾ measure fresh lemon
    juice
¾ measure fresh orange
    juice
3½ measures strong fruit
    tea, chilled
orange and lemon slices
    and a mint sprig, to
    decorate

Put a handful of ice cubes with
the tequila, rum, Cointreau,
sugar syrup, fruit juices and tea
into a cocktail shaker and shake
vigorously. Strain into a sling
glass filled with fresh ice cubes.
Decorate with orange and
lemon slices and a mint sprig.

Did you know?
One of the best teas to use as a base
for this refreshing drink is a mixed
berry tea. Its essential fruitiness
blends very well with the citrus
juices in Texas Tea.`

Jalisco Swizzle

4–5 ice cubes, plus crushed
ice to serve
3 dashes Angostura bitters
¾ measure tequila gold
¾ measure golden rum
1¼ measures fresh lime
juice
¾ measure passion fruit
juice
2 teaspoons sugar syrup
soda water, to top up
lime slice and mint sprig,
to decorate

Put the ice cubes with the
bitters, tequila, rum, lime juice
and sugar syrup into a cocktail
shaker and shake vigorously.
Strain into a highball glass
filled with crushed ice. Top up
with soda and stir briefly until a
frost forms. Decorate with a
lime slice and a mint sprig.

Mexicana

8–10 ice cubes
1¼ measures tequila
¾ measure framboise
liqueur
¾ measure fresh lemon
juice
3½ measures pineapple
juice
pineapple wedge and lemon
slice, to decorate

Put half the ice cubes with the
tequila, framboise and fruit
juices into a cocktail shaker and
shake vigorously for about 10
seconds. Pour over the
remaining ice cubes in a large
highball glass and decorate
with a pineapple wedge and a
lemon slice.

Did you know?

Framboise is an *alcool blanc*, a fruit
liqueur (in this case raspberry)
which is stored in glass rather than
wood and so does not acquire any
colour from the cask while it is in
the process of maturing.

Tijuana Sling

ice cubes
1¼ measures tequila
¾ measure crème de cassis
¾ measure fresh lime juice
2 dashes Peychaud bitters
3½ measures dry ginger ale
lime slice and blackcurrants
or blueberries, to
decorate

Put some ice cubes with the
tequila, crème de cassis, lime
juice and bitters into a cocktail
shaker and shake vigorously.
Pour into a large sling glass,
then top up with dry ginger
ale. Decorate with a lime slice
and some berries.

Tijuana Sling ▶

Brooklyn Bomber

5 ice cubes, crushed
1 measure tequila
½ measure Cointreau
½ measure cherry brandy
½ measure Galliano
1 measure lemon juice
orange slice and cocktail
    cherry, to decorate

Put half the crushed ice into
a cocktail shaker and add
the tequila, Cointreau, cherry
brandy, Galliano and lemon
juice. Shake to mix. Pour
over the remaining ice in a
hurricane glass. Decorate with
the orange slice and cherry
and serve with straws.

Tequila de Coco

crushed ice
1 measure tequila
1 measure fresh lemon juice
1 measure coconut syrup
3 dashes Maraschino
    liqueur
lemon slice, to decorate

Put some crushed ice into a
blender and add the tequila,
lemon juice, coconut syrup and
Maraschino. Blend for a few
seconds, then pour into a
Collins glass and decorate
with a lemon slice.

Rooster Booster

ice cubes
1¼ measures tequila
6 measures fresh
    grapefruit juice
1 tablespoon grenadine
3½ measures soda water
lime slice and cocktail
    cherry, to decorate

Put some ice cubes into a large
highball glass. Pour in the
tequila, grapefruit juice and
grenadine, stir gently, then top
up with soda water. Decorate
with a lime slice and a cherry.

Tequila Sunrise

ice cubes
2 measures tequila
4 measures orange juice
2 teaspoons grenadine
orange slices, to decorate

Put some ice cubes with the tequila and orange juice into a cocktail shaker and shake to mix. Strain into a highball glass filled with ice cubes. Slowly pour in the grenadine and allow it to settle. Decorate with an orange slice.

Did you know?
The Tequila Sunrise is one of the cocktails made popular during the Prohibition, when the orange juice helped to disguise the taste of the raw alcohol.

South for the Summer

2 teaspoons grenadine
crushed ice
2 measures tequila
3 measures orange juice
4 pineapple chunks
pineapple leaf and orange rind, to decorate

Spoon the grenadine into a highball glass. Put some crushed ice with the tequila, orange juice and pineapple chunks into a food processor or blender and blend until slushy. Pour the mixture over the grenadine, decorate with a pineapple leaf and an orange twist and stir just before serving.

Agave Julep

8 torn mint leaves
1 tablespoon sugar syrup
1¼ measures tequila gold
1¼ measures fresh lime juice
crushed ice
lime wedge and mint sprig, to decorate

Muddle the mint leaves with the sugar syrup in a highball glass. Add the tequila and lime juice, fill the glass with crushed ice and stir vigorously to mix. Decorate with a lime wedge and a mint sprig.

Border Crossing

ice cubes
1½ measures gold tequila
1 measure fresh lime juice
1 measure clear honey
4 dashes orange bitters
3 measures dry ginger ale
blueberries and lime
    wedges, to decorate

Put some ice cubes with the tequila, lime juice, honey and bitters in a cocktail shaker and shake well. Pour into a highball glass and top up with the dry ginger ale. Decorate with blueberries and lime wedges.

Beckoning Lady

6–8 ice cubes
2 measures tequila
4 measures passion
    fruit juice
1–2 teaspoons Galliano
cocktail cherries, to
    decorate

Fill a hurricane or highball glass with the ice. Using the back of a bar spoon, slowly add the tequila and passion fruit juice and stir well to mix. Float the Galliano on top in a layer about 1 cm (½ inch) deep and decorate with cherries.

Mexican Mule

1 lime
1 dash sugar syrup
crushed ice
1 measure José Cuervo
    Gold tequila
1 measure Kahlúa
dry ginger ale, to top up

Cut the lime into slices, put them into a highball glass and muddle with the sugar syrup. Half-fill the glass with crushed ice and add the tequila and Kahlúa. Stir well, then top up with dry ginger ale.

Mexicola

4 lime wedges
crushed ice
1¼ measures tequila
6 measures cola

Muddle the lime wedges in a large highball glass. Fill the glass with crushed ice, then pour in the tequila and cola. Stir gently, lifting the lime wedges through the drink.

Alleluia

ice cubes
¾ measure tequila
½ measure blue Curaçao
2 teaspoons Maraschino
   syrup
1 dash egg white
¾ measure fresh lemon
   juice
3½ measures bitter lemon
lemon slice, cocktail
   cherry and mint sprig,
   to decorate

Put 4–5 ice cubes with the tequila, Curaçao, Maraschino syrup, egg white and lemon juice into a cocktail shaker and shake vigorously. Strain into a large highball glass filled with ice cubes. Top up with the bitter lemon and stir gently. Decorate with a lemon slice, a cherry and a mint sprig.

Did you know?
For maraschino syrup, use the syrup from the jar of Maraschino cherries.

Acapulco Bliss

4–5 ice cubes
¾ measure tequila
1 tablespoon Pisang Ambon
   (banana liqueur)
2 teaspoons Galliano
¾ measure fresh lemon juice
¾ measure single cream
3½ measures passion fruit
   juice
lemon slices, pineapple
   wedge and mint sprig,
   to decorate

Put the ice cubes with the tequila, Pisang Ambon, Galliano, lemon juice, cream and passion fruit juice into a cocktail shaker and shake vigorously. Pour into a large sling glass and decorate with lemon slices, a pineapple wedge and a mint sprig.

Mexican Bulldog

ice cubes
¾ measure tequila
¾ measure Kahlúa
1¼ measures single cream
3½ measures cola
drinking chocolate powder,
    to decorate

Put some ice cubes into a
highball glass. Pour in the
tequila, Kahlúa and cream, then
top up with the cola. Stir gently
and serve decorated with
drinking chocolate powder.

Brave Bull

ice cubes
¾ measure tequila
¾ measure Kahlúa

Fill an old-fashioned glass with
ice cubes. Pour in the tequila
and Kahlúa and stir gently.

Did you know?
To turn a Brave Bull into a Brown
Cow, add 1¼ measures single
cream and stir to blend it in. To turn
a Brave Bull into a Raging Bull, add
1 teaspoon flaming Sambuca.

Sombrero

4–5 ice cubes
¾ measure tequila gold
¾ measure white crème
    de cacao
3½ measures single cream
grated nutmeg, to decorate

Put the ice cubes into a cocktail
shaker. Pour in the tequila,
crème de cacao and cream
and shake vigorously for 10
seconds. Strain into a chilled
cocktail glass. Sprinkle with
grated nutmeg.

Floreciente

1 orange slice
fine sea salt
crushed ice
1¼ measures tequila gold
¾ measure fresh lemon
    juice
¾ measure fresh blood
    orange juice
blood orange wedge,
    to decorate

Frost the rim of a large
old-fashioned glass by
moistening with an orange
slice then pressing the glass
into salt. Fill it with crushed
ice. Pour the tequila, Cointreau,
lemon juice and blood
orange juice into a cocktail
shaker, shake vigorously for
10 seconds, then strain into
the prepared glass. Decorate
with a blood orange wedge.

Pink Cadillac Convertible

3 lime wedges
fine sea salt
ice cubes
1¼ measures gold tequila
½ measure cranberry juice
¾ measure Grand Marnier
lime wedge, to decorate

Frost the rim of a large old-
fashioned glass by moistening
with a lime wedge, then pressing
into salt. Fill the glass with ice
cubes. Pour the tequila and
cranberry juice into a cocktail
shaker. Squeeze over the juice
from the remaining lime wedges,
pressing the rind to release its
oils. Drop the wedges into the
shaker. Add 4–5 ice cubes and
shake vigorously for 10 seconds,
then strain into the glass. Drizzle
the Grand Marnier over the top
and decorate with lime wedges.

Desert Daisy

crushed ice
1 measure tequila
1¼ measures fresh lime
    juice
2 teaspoons sugar syrup
1 tablespoon Fraise de Bois
blackberry and strawberry,
    lime and orange wedges
    and mint sprig, to
    decorate

Half-fill a large old-fashioned
glass with crushed ice. Pour in
the tequila, lime juice and sugar
syrup and stir gently until a
frost forms. Add more crushed
ice then float the Fraise de Bois
on top. Decorate with a
blackberry, a strawberry, a lime
wedge, an orange wedge and a
mint sprig.

Forest Fruit

1 lime wedge
soft brown sugar
2 blackberries, plus extra
　to decorate
2 raspberries, plus extra
　to decorate
2 teaspoons Chambord
2 teaspoons crème de mure
1¼ measures tequila
2 teaspoons Cointreau
1¼ measures fresh lemon
　juice
crushed ice
lemon slices, to decorate

Frost the rim of an old-fashioned glass by moistening with the lime wedge and pressing into brown sugar. Drop the blackberries and raspberries into the glass and muddle to a pulp. Stir in the Chambord and crème de mure. Pour in the tequila, Cointreau and lemon juice, fill with crushed ice and stir gently, lifting the muddled berries from the bottom of the glass. Decorate with lemon slices and a blackberry and a raspberry.

Baja Sour

4–5 ice cubes
1¼ measures tequila gold
2 teaspoons sugar syrup
1¼ measures fresh lemon
　juice
2 dashes orange bitters
½ egg white
1 tablespoon Amontillado
　sherry
lemon slices and orange
　rind spiral, to decorate

Put the ice cubes with the tequila, sugar syrup, lemon juice, bitters and egg white into a cocktail shaker and shake vigorously. Pour into a large sour glass and drizzle over the sherry. Decorate with lemon slices and an orange rind spiral.

Ruby Rita

1¼ measures fresh pink
　grapefruit juice
fine sea salt
ice cubes
1¼ measures tequila gold
¾ measure Cointreau
pink grapefruit wedge,
　to decorate

Frost the rim of an old-fashioned glass by moistening with some of the pink grapefruit juice and pressing into salt. Fill the glass with ice cubes. Pour the tequila, Cointreau and the remaining pink grapefruit juice into a cocktail shaker, fill with more ice and shake vigorously. Strain into the prepared glass and decorate with a pink grapefruit wedge.

Ruby Rita ▶

Batanga

1 Mexican lime
rock salt
ice cubes
2 measures Tequileno
    Blanco tequila
Mexican cola, to top up

Cut the tip off the lime and make a slit in its side. Dip in the salt and run it around the edge of an old-fashioned glass. Fill the glass with ice cubes and add the tequila. Squeeze out half the lime juice, then with the knife used to cut the lime, stir the drink while topping up with Mexican cola.

Cobalt Margarita

1 lime wedge
fine sea salt
4–5 ice cubes
1¼ measures tequila
2 teaspoons Cointreau
½ measure blue Curaçao
¾ measure fresh lime juice
¾ measure fresh grapefruit
    juice
lime rind spiral, to decorate

Frost the rim of a chilled cocktail glass by moistening with a lime wedge then pressing into salt. Put the ice cubes with the tequila, Cointreau, blue Curaçao, fruit juices into a cocktail shaker and shake vigorously for 10 seconds. Strain into the prepared glass. Decorate with a lime rind spiral.

Did you know?
The 150-year-old Cointreau, unlike Grand Marnier, is a clear orange-flavoured liqueur, which has a balance of sweet and bitter orange tones.

Passion Fruit Margarita

lime wedge
coarse sea salt
ice cubes
1½ measures gold tequila
1 measure Cointreau
1 teaspoon passion fruit
    syrup
1 measure fresh lime juice
pulp and seeds of 1 passion
    fruit
lime wedges, to decorate

Frost the rim of a margarita glass by moistening with a lime wedge and pressing into the salt. Put some ice cubes with the tequila, Cointreau, passion fruit syrup, lime juice and half the passion fruit pulp into a cocktail shaker and shake well. Double strain into the prepared glass. Add the remaining passion fruit pulp and decorate with lime wedges.

Margarita

1 lime wedge
rock salt
ice cubes
2 measures Herrudura
    Reposado tequila
1 measure lime juice
1 measure Triple Sec
lime slice, to decorate

Frost the rim of a coupette glass
by moistening with the lime
wedge, then pressing into the
salt. Put some ice cubes with
the tequila, lime juice and
Triple Sec into a cocktail
shaker. Shake well. Strain into
the prepared glass. Decorate
with a lime slice.

Grand Margarita

1 lime wedge, plus
    1 to decorate
rock salt
ice cubes
1½ measures silver tequila
1 measure Grand Marnier
1 measure lime juice

Frost the rim of a coupette glass
by moistening with the lime
wedge then pressing into the
salt. Put some ice cubes with
the tequila, Grand Marnier and
lime juice into a cocktail shaker
and shake well. Double strain
into the prepared glass and
decorate with a lime wedge.

Cadillac

3 lime wedges
fine sea salt
1¼ measures tequila gold
½ measure Cointreau
1¼ measures fresh lime
    juice
4–5 ice cubes
2 teaspoons Grand Marnier
lime slice, to decorate

Frost the rim of a chilled
cocktail glass by moistening
with a lime wedge, then
pressing into the salt. Pour the
tequila, Cointreau and lime
juice into a cocktail shaker.
Squeeze over the juice from
the remaining lime wedges,
pressing the rind to release
its oils. Drop the wedges into
the shaker. Add the ice cubes
and shake vigorously for 10
seconds, then strain into the
prepared glass. Drizzle the
Grand Marnier over the top
and decorate with a lime slice.

Maracuja

1 fresh ripe passion fruit
4–5 ice cubes
1¼ measures tequila gold
1 tablespoon Creole Shrub
¾ measure fresh lime juice
2 teaspoons Cointreau
1 teaspoon passion fruit
    syrup
physalis (Cape gooseberry),
    to decorate

Cut the passion fruit in half and
scoop the flesh into a cocktail
shaker. Add the ice cubes with
the tequila, Creole Shrub, lime
juice, Cointreau and passion
fruit syrup and shake
vigorously for 10 seconds.
Strain through a fine sieve
into a chilled cocktail glass.
Decorate with a physalis.

South of the Border

4–5 ice cubes
1¼ measures tequila
¾ measure Kahlúa
1¼ measures fresh
    lime juice

Put the ice cubes with the
tequila, Kahlúa and lime juice
into a cocktail shaker and shake
vigorously for 10 seconds.
Strain into a chilled cocktail
glass.

Ananas and Coco

crushed ice
1¼ measures tequila gold
¾ measure coconut syrup
1 large pineapple chunk
1¼ measures pineapple
    juice
pineapple wedge, to
    decorate

Put a handful of crushed ice
with the tequila, coconut syrup
and pineapple juice into a food
processor or blender and blend
for 20 seconds. Pour into a wine
goblet. Decorate with a
pineapple wedge.

Did you know?
Tequila gold, as its name indicates,
is golden in colour, having been
aged in oak casks for between 2
and 4 years, as opposed to tequila
silver, which is clear and young.
Creole Shrub is a rum-based orange
liqueur from Martinique.

Viva Maria

ice cubes, plus crushed ice
    to serve
1 measure tequila
½ measure fresh lime juice
¼ measure Maraschino
    liqueur
½ teaspoon grenadine
½ egg white
lemon and lime slices
    and a cocktail cherry,
    to decorate

Put the ice cubes into a cocktail
shaker and pour over the
tequila, lime juice, Maraschino,
grenadine and egg white. Shake
well and strain into a wide
Champagne glass filled with
crushed ice. Decorate with
lemon and lime slices and a
cocktail cherry.

Sour Apple

4–5 ice cubes
1¼ measures tequila
2 teaspoons Cointreau
1 tablespoon apple
    schnapps
¾ measure fresh lime juice
¾ measure dry apple juice
Granny Smith apple wedge,
    to decorate

Put the ice cubes with the
tequila, Cointreau, schnapps
and fruit juices into a cocktail
shaker and shake vigorously for
10 seconds. Strain into a chilled
cocktail glass. Decorate with an
apple wedge.

Azteca

crushed ice, plus 4–5 ice
    cubes to serve
1 measure tequila
juice of ½ lime
½ teaspoon sugar syrup
1 small mango, skinned
    and stoned
½ lime slice, to decorate

Put a handful of crushed ice
into a food processor or blender
with the tequila, lime juice,
sugar syrup and mango and
blend briefly. Strain over the ice
cubes in a large cocktail glass.
Decorate with a lime slice half
and serve with short straws.

Earthquake

3 measures crushed ice
1½ measures tequila
1 teaspoon grenadine
2 strawberries, hulled
1–2 dashes orange bitters
lime slice and strawberry,
    to decorate

Put the crushed ice with the
tequila, grenadine, strawberries
and bitters in a food processor
or blender and process at high
speed for 15 seconds. Strain
into a cocktail glass and
decorate with a lime slice
and a strawberry.

Honey Water

4–5 ice cubes
1¼ measures tequila gold
¾ measure sweet vermouth
3 dashes Angostura bitters
3 dashes Peychaud bitters
2 teaspoons Grand Marnier
cocktail cherry and orange
    rind spiral, to decorate

Put the ice cubes into a mixing
glass, pour in the tequila,
vermouth and bitters and stir
gently for 10 seconds. Put the
Grand Marnier into a chilled
cocktail glass, swirl to coat the
inside of the glass, then tip it
out. Stir the contents of the
mixing glass again for
10 seconds then strain into
the cocktail glass. Decorate
with a cherry and an orange
rind spiral.

Mad Dog

4–5 ice cubes
1 measure tequila
1 measure crème de banane
1 measure crème de cacao
juice of ½ lime
lime slice, banana slice
    and cocktail cherry,
    to decorate

Put the ice cubes into a cocktail
shaker. Pour the tequila, crème
de banane, crème de cacao and
lime juice over the ice and
shake until a frost forms. Strain
into a chilled cocktail glass and
decorate with a lime and a
banana slice and cherry
impaled on a cocktail stick.

Dirty Sanchez

ice cubes
2 teaspoons Noilly Prat
2 measures gold tequila
  (preferably Anejo)
2 teaspoons brine from a jar
  of black olives
2 black olives, to decorate

Fill a mixing glass with ice
cubes and add the vermouth.
Stir to coat the ice, then discard
the excess vermouth. Add the
tequila and brine and stir until
thoroughly chilled. Strain into
a chilled cocktail glass and
decorate with black olives.

Pancho Villa

4–5 ice cubes
1 measure tequila
½ measure Tia Maria
1 teaspoon Cointreau

Put the ice cubes into a cocktail
shaker and pour in the tequila,
Tia Maria and Cointreau. Shake
until a frost forms, then strain
into a chilled cocktail glass.

Acapulco

crushed ice
1 measure tequila
1 measure white rum
2 measures pineapple juice
1 measure grapefruit juice
1 measure coconut milk

Put some crushed ice into a
cocktail shaker and pour in the
tequila, rum, fruit juices and
coconut milk. Shake to mix,
then pour into a hurricane
glass. Serve with straws.

Silk Stocking

drinking chocolate powder
4–5 ice cubes
¾ measure tequila
¾ measure white crème
   de cacao
3½ measures single cream
2 teaspoons grenadine

Frost the rim of a chilled
cocktail glass by dipping into
water, then pressing into the
drinking chocolate powder. Put
the ice cubes with the tequila,
crème de cacao, cream and
grenadine into a cocktail
shaker. Shake vigorously for
10 seconds, then strain into the
prepared glass.

Thigh High

3 strawberries, hulled
1 teaspoon strawberry
   syrup
4–5 ice cubes
1 measure tequila
1 measure dark crème
   de cacao
1½ measures single cream
1 strawberry dipped in
   cocoa powder, to decorate

Muddle the strawberries and
strawberry syrup in a cocktail
shaker. Add the ice cubes with
the tequila, crème de cacao and
cream and shake to mix. Strain
into a large, chilled cocktail glass
and decorate with a strawberry
dipped in cocoa powder.

Did you know?
Crème de cacao, the chocolate
liqueur, comes in two versions, dark
and white. Choose according to how
you want your drink to look.
Combining the dark version in a
Sombrero with tequila gold and
cream would result in a subtle
coffee-coloured drink.

Frostbite

4–5 ice cubes
1 measure tequila
1 measure double cream
1 measure white crème
   de cacao
½ measure white crème
   de menthe
drinking chocolate powder,
   to decorate

Put the ice cubes into a cocktail
shaker. Pour in the tequila,
cream, crème de cacao and
crème de menthe and shake
vigorously for 10 seconds.
Strain into a chilled cocktail
glass. Sprinkle with drinking
chocolate powder.

Chapala

1¼ measures tequila
¾ measure Cointreau
¾ measure fresh
    lemon juice
¾ measure fresh
    orange juice
2 teaspoons grenadine
orange rind spiral,
    to decorate

Pour the tequila, Cointreau
and fruit juices into a cocktail
shaker. Add the grenadine
and shake vigorously for
10 seconds, then strain into a
chilled cocktail glass. Decorate
with an orange rind spiral.

Off-shore

crushed ice
1 measure white rum
1 measure gold tequila
6 mint leaves
2 pineapple chunks
3 measures pineapple juice
1 measure single cream
mint sprigs, to decorate

Put some crushed ice with the
rum, tequila, mint leaves,
pineapple chunks, pineapple
juice and cream in a food
processor or blender and blend
until slushy. Transfer to
a hurricane glass and decorate
with mint sprigs.

Rude Cosmopolitan

ice cubes
1½ measures gold tequila
1 measure Cointreau
1 measure cranberry juice
½ measure fresh lime juice
flamed orange rind twist,
    to decorate

Put some ice cubes into a
cocktail shaker, add the tequila,
Cointreau, and fruit juices and
shake well. Strain into a chilled
Martini glass and decorate with
a flamed orange rind twist.

Did you know?
To make a flamed orange rind twist,
cut a large, wide piece of orange
rind and make sure there is no
white pith attached. Hold in one
hand, rind side down, about 10 cm
(4 in) above the drink and a long,
lighted match or candle in the other.
Pinch the rind firmly so that the oils
spray into the flame and ignite onto
the drink.

Tequini

ice cubes
3 dashes orange bitters
3 measures tequila blanco
2 teaspoons dry French
    vermouth, preferably
    Noilly Prat
black olive, to decorate

Fill a mixing glass with ice
cubes, then add the bitters and
tequila. Stir gently for
10 seconds. Put the vermouth
in a chilled cocktail glass and
swirl to coat the inside, then
tip it out. Stir the bitters and
tequila for a further 10 seconds
and strain into the cocktail
glass. Decorate with a black
olive in the glass.

Pale Original

ice cubes
2 measures gold tequila
½ measure ginger syrup
½ measure fresh lime juice
1 measure guava juice
lime wedges, to decorate

Put some ice cubes with the
tequila, ginger syrup and fruit
juices into a cocktail shaker and
shake well. Strain into a chilled
cocktail glass.

Sloe Tequila

ice cubes
1 measure tequila
2 tablespoons sloe gin
2 tablespoons lime juice
cucumber peel spiral,
    to decorate

Put some ice cubes with the
tequila, sloe gin and lime juice
into a cocktail shaker and shake
well. Strain into a cocktail glass
and fill up with ice cubes.
Decorate with the cucumber
peel spiral.

Tequila Slammer

1 measure gold tequila
1 measure Champagne

Pour the tequila into a shot glass. Slowly top up with Champagne. Cover the top of the glass with the palm of your hand to seal the contents inside and grip it with your fingers. Briskly pick up the glass and slam it down on to a surface to make the drink fizz, then quickly gulp it down in one, while still fizzing.

Mockingbird

ice cubes
1¼ measures tequila
¾ measure green crème de menthe
1¼ measures fresh lime juice
lemon rind spiral, to decorate

Put some ice cubes with the tequila, crème de menthe and lime juice into a cocktail shaker and shake vigorously for about 10 seconds. Strain into a chilled cocktail glass. Decorate with a lemon rind spiral.

Flat Liner

¾ measure gold tequila
4 drops Tabasco sauce
¾ measure Sambuca

First pour the tequila into a shot glass. Using the back of a bar spoon, slowly float the Tabasco over the tequila. Pour the Sambuca over the Tabasco in the same way.

Passion Spawn

ice cubes
1 measure silver tequila
1 dash Triple Sec
1 dash fresh lime juice
1 passion fruit

Put some ice cubes with the tequila, Triple Sec and lime juice into a cocktail shaker and shake well. Strain into a chilled shot glass. Cut the passion fruit in half and squeeze over the shot before serving.

Did you know?
This provides a real assault on the taste buds, with tequila, Triple Sec and lime hiding beneath a layer of fresh passion fruit.

Sangrita

ice cubes
1 measure tomato juice
1 dash Worcestershire sauce
2 drops Tabasco sauce
cracked black pepper
celery salt
1 lime wedge
1½ measures tequila

Put some ice cubes with the tomato juice, Worcestershire and Tabasco sauce, cracked pepper and celery salt into a cocktail shaker and shake briefly. Strain into a large shot glass. Serve the tequila in an identical glass alongside the spiced tomato shot.

Raspberry Beret

½ measure light crème de cacao
1 measure chilled gold tequila
1 plump raspberry

Pour the crème de cacao into a shot glass. Using the back of a bar spoon, slowly float the tequila over the crème de cacao. Slowly lower the raspberry into the drink – it will settle between the 2 spirits.

Raspberry Beret ▶

Wine and Champagne

Wine and Champagne (which is in fact a sparkling wine) are produced from grapes. Wine has probably been made by man since before recorded history. While wine is produced all over the world from a huge range of grapes, true Champagne can only claim that name if it has been produced in the Champagne region of France. The story goes that Champagne was invented by a monk who kept accidentally ending up with bubbles in his wine. Champagne can be made with both white and black grapes, although only three grape varieties are used. White wine can also be produced from black grapes; the difference occurs due to the skins being left in while red wine is fermenting.

Classic Champagne cocktails include Buck's Fizz and Bellini. Wine doesn't feature so heavily on cocktail lists, but you might like to try a White Sangria, and Christmas just wouldn't be Christmas without a glass of Glühwein.

Lime Fizz

1 lime wedge
1 measure lime vodka
1 measure orange juice
ice cubes
Champagne, to top up
Lime rind twists, to decorate

Squeeze the lime wedge into
a cocktail shaker and add the
vodka and orange juice with
some ice cubes. Shake very
briefly and double strain into
a chilled Champagne flute.
Top up with Champagne and
decorate with lime rind twists.

Cheshire Cat

4–5 ice cubes
1 measure brandy
1 measure sweet vermouth
1 measure fresh orange
    juice
Champagne, to top up
orange rind strip, to
    decorate
orange rind spiral, to
    decorate

Put the ice cubes into a mixing
glass. Pour the brandy, vermouth
and orange juice over the ice
and stir to mix. Strain into a
Champagne flute and top up
with Champagne. Squeeze the
zest from the orange rind over
the drink and decorate with an
orange rind spiral.

Grand Mimosa

1 measure Grand Marnier
2 measures orange juice,
    chilled
chilled Champagne, to
    top up

Pour the Grand Marnier and
orange juice into a Champagne
flute and top up with chilled
Champagne.

Did you know?
This is a Buck's Fizz (opposite) with
a difference! It was created in 1925
at the Ritz Hotel in Paris and named
after the mimosa plant – probably
because of its trembling leaves,
which are rather like the gentle fizz
of this mixture.

Grandaddy Mimosa

ice cubes
1 measure Havana Club
   3-year-old rum
1 measure orange juice
½ measure fresh lemon
   juice
chilled Champagne,
   to top up
orange rind twist,
   to decorate
1 dash grenadine

Put some ice cubes with the
rum and fruit juices into a
shaker with some ice cubes and
shake to mix. Strain into a large
Champagne flute, then top
up with chilled Champagne.
Decorate with an orange rind
twist and drop in the grenadine.

Buck's Fizz

2 measures chilled
   orange juice
6 measures chilled
   Champagne

Pour the chilled orange juice
into a cocktail glass and add
the chilled Champagne.

Did you know?
Chilled orange juice and
Champagne make up this
celebratory drink. If you're making
large quantities for a party in a jug,
don't forget to leave room for the
Champagne to fizz up.

Buck's Twizz

1 measure chilled
   orange juice
½ measure Maraschino
   liqueur
1 measure Absolut
   Mandrin vodka
chilled Champagne, to
   top up
rindless pink grapefruit
   slice, to decorate

Pour the orange juice and
Maraschino into a chilled
Champagne saucer, then add
the vodka and Champagne at
the same time (this prevents
excessive fizzing). Decorate with
a rindless pink grapefruit slice.

Bellini

2 measures peach juice
4 measures chilled
   Champagne
1 dash grenadine (optional)
peach slice, to decorate

Mix the peach juice and
chilled Champagne in a large
Champagne flute with a dash
of grenadine, if using. Decorate
with a peach slice.

Did you know?
Originating in Harry's Bar in Venice,
the original Bellini was made with
prosecco (an Italian sparkling wine)
and white peach purée.

Mango Bellini

3 measures mango juice
pink Champagne, to top up

Pour the mango juice into a
Champagne flute and top up
with pink Champagne. Stir
gently to mix and serve
immediately.

Secret Smile

lightly beaten egg white
granulated sugar
1 measure orange juice
½ measure Galliano
chilled Champagne or
   sparkling dry white wine,
   to top up
orange rind spiral, to
   decorate

Frost the rim of a Champagne
flute or tall glass by dipping
into the egg white, then the
sugar. Pour in the orange juice
and Galliano and top up with
chilled Champagne or
sparkling wine. Decorate the
rim with the orange rind spiral.

California Dreaming

ice cubes
2 dashes kirsch
3 measures pineapple juice
1 dash lemon juice
chilled Champagne, to
    top up
pineapple wedge, to
    decorate

Put some ice cubes with the kirsch and fruit juices into a food processor or blender and blend for 30 seconds. Pour into a wine glass and top up with chilled Champagne. Decorate with a pineapple wedge.

Champagne Romanov Fizz

2 ice cubes
8–10 ripe strawberries,
    hulled
4 measures orange juice
4 measures Champagne
strawberry slice and mint
    sprig, to decorate

Put 1 ice cube with the strawberries and orange juice into a blender or food processor and blend until smooth. Put the remaining ice cube into a tall glass and add the strawberry liquid. Top up with the Champagne. Stir briskly and serve immediately.

Did you know?
Replace the strawberries with ripe raspberries. Sieve the drink before serving to remove the pips.

Caribbean Champagne

1 tablespoon light rum
1 tablespoon crème de
    banane
1 dash Angostura bitters
Champagne, to top up
banana slice, pineapple
    slice and cocktail cherry,
    to decorate

Pour the rum, crème de banane and bitters into a chilled Champagne flute. Top up with Champagne and stir gently. Decorate with the banana, pineapple and cherry, all speared on a cocktail stick.

La Seine Fizz

1 measure Cognac
½ measure Fraise de Bois
½ measure lemon juice
1 dash orange bitters
2 strawberries, hulled and
    chopped
sugar syrup, to taste
3 measures Champagne
½ measure Grand Marnier
strawberry wedge and mint
    sprig, to decorate

Put the Cognac, Fraise de Bois, lemon juice, bitters and strawberries into a cocktail shaker with some sugar syrup to taste. Shake and strain into a Champagne glass. Top up with the Champagne and pour the Grand Marnier over the top. Decorate with a strawberry wedge and a mint sprig.

Carlton

ice cubes
3 measures orange juice
2 tablespoons Grand
    Marnier
1 egg white
2–3 dashes peach bitters
Champagne, to top up
cocktail cherry, to decorate

Put some ice cubes into a cocktail shaker and pour over the Grand Marnier, egg white and bitters. Shake very well. Strain into a Champagne saucer, top up with Champagne and stir gently. Decorate with a cherry.

Eve

several drops Pernod
1 tablespoon Cognac
2 teaspoons sugar
2 teaspoons Curaçao
pink Champagne, to top up

Add the Pernod drops to a Champagne saucer; turn to coat the inside of the glass. Pour in the Cognac. Soak the sugar in the Curaçao until the sugar has dissolved, then add to the Cognac and stir gently. Top up the glass with pink Champagne.

Slinky Mink

½ measure raspberry purée
1 dash sugar syrup
2 teaspoons lime juice
Champagne, to top up
lime rind twist, to decorate

Build the raspberry purée,
sugar syrup and lime juice in
the bottom of a chilled flute.
Top up with Champagne, stir
lightly and decorate with a lime
rind twist.

Kitsch Revolt

ice cubes
1 measure Absolut
   Kurant vodka
½ measure strawberry
   purée
4 measures chilled
   Champagne

Put some ice cubes with the
vodka and strawberry purée
into a shaker and shake briefly.
Strain into a Martini glass, then
top up with chilled Champagne
and stir well.

Did you know?
The strawberry purée for this twist
can be bought from good grocery
stores or made by liquidizing hulled
ripe strawberries.

Lush Crush

2 strawberries, hulled
1 dash sugar syrup
2 lime wedges
1 measure Absolut
   Kurant vodka
ice cubes
Champagne, to top up
strawberry slices, to
   decorate

Muddle the strawberries, sugar
syrup and lime wedges into a
cocktail shaker. Add the vodka
and some ice cubes. Shake and
double strain into a chilled
Champagne flute. Top up with
Champagne and decorate
with a strawberry slice.

ChamPino

ice cubes
1 measure Campari
1¼ measures sweet
    vermouth
Champagne, to top up
lemon rind twist, to
    decorate

Put some ice cubes with the
Campari and vermouth into
a cocktail shaker and shake.
Strain into a chilled Martini
glass. Top up with chilled
Champagne and decorate
with a lemon rind twist.

Celebration Cocktail

1 lemon wedge
caster sugar
ice cubes
1 measure brandy
1 dash Bénédictine
1 dash crème de mure
chilled Champagne, to
    top up

Frost the rim of a Champagne
flute by moistening with the
lemon wedge then pressing into
the sugar. Put some ice cubes
into a cocktail shaker and add
the brandy, Bénédictine and
crème de mure. Shake well,
strain into the prepared glass
and top up with Champagne.

Ritz Fizz I

1 dash blue Curaçao
1 dash lemon juice
1 dash Amaretto di Saronno
Champagne, to top up
lemon rind spiral, to
    decorate

Pour the Curaçao, lemon juice
and Amaretto into a glass and
top up with Champagne. Stir
gently to mix and decorate
with a lemon rind spiral.

Ritz Fizz II

ice cubes
½ measure crème de cassis
½ measure Poire William
chilled Champagne, to
    top up
pear slices, peeled, to
    decorate

Put some ice cubes with the
crème de cassis and Poire
William into a mixing glass
and stir to mix well. Strain into
a Champagne flute and top
up with chilled Champagne.
Decorate with peeled pear slices.

Did you know?
The blend of pear and blackcurrant
liqueurs as the base of this
delicious Champagne cocktail make
it a little too easy to drink!

Kir Champagne Royale

1 teaspoon vodka
2 teaspoons crème de cassis
Champagne, to top up

Put the vodka and crème de
cassis into a Champagne flute.
Top up with Champagne.

Man in the Moon

ice cubes
1 measure vodka
½ measure apricot brandy
½ measure lemon juice
2 dashes grenadine
chilled Champagne or
    sparkling wine, to top up

Put some ice cubes with the
vodka, apricot brandy, lemon
juice and grenadine into a
cocktail shaker and shake well.
Strain into a Champagne glass
and top up with chilled
Champagne (or sparkling wine).

Bubble Berry

2 raspberries
2 blackberries, plus extra
  to decorate
½ measure framboise
  liqueur
½ measure crème de mure
3 measures Champagne

Muddle the raspberries and
blackberries in a Champagne
glass. Add the framboise and
the crème de mure. Top up with
the Champagne. Decorate the
glass with a blackberry and
serve immediately.

The Classic's Classic

1 sugar cube
2 dashes Angostura bitters
1 measure Grand Marnier
4 measures chilled
  Champagne
orange rind, to decorate

Saturate the sugar cube with
the bitters, then drop it into
a Champagne flute. Add the
Grand Marnier, then top up
with the chilled Champagne.
Drop the orange rind in the
drink to decorate.

Gorgeous Grace

ice cubes
1 measure brandy
½ measure Cointreau
chilled Champagne, or
  sparkling dry white wine,
  to top up
orange slice, to decorate

Put some ice cubes with the
brandy and Cointreau into
a mixing glass. Pour into a
Champagne glass and top up
with chilled Champagne or
sparkling wine. Decorate
with orange slice.

Did you know?
To make Gorgeous Grace even more
gorgeous, try using pink Champagne
or sparkling wine for an additional
flavour and colour dimension.

Classic Champagne Cocktail

1 sugar cube
1–2 dashes Angostura
   bitters
1 measure brandy
chilled Champagne, to
   top up
orange slice, to decorate

Saturate the sugar cube with
the bitters, then drop it into a
chilled cocktail or Champagne
glass. Add the brandy, then top
up with chilled Champagne.
Decorate with an orange slice.

Head-over-heels

4–5 ice cubes
juice of 1 lime
3 measures vodka
sugar cube
3 drops Angostura bitters
Champagne, to top up

Put the ice cubes into a
cocktail shaker. Pour the lime
juice and vodka over the ice
and shake until a frost forms.
Drop a sugar cube into a glass
and shake the bitters over it.
Strain the contents of the
shaker into the glass and top
up with Champagne.

Cavendish

chopped ice
2 drops Angostura bitters
2 measures vodka
chilled Champagne, to
   top up
lemon rind twist, to
   decorate

Fill a highball glass with
chopped ice. Shake the bitters
over the ice. Pour in the vodka
and top up with chilled
Champagne. Squeeze the
lemon rind twist over the
drink and drop it in.

E = mc²

4–5 crushed ice cubes
2 measures Southern
   Comfort
1 measure fresh lemon juice
½ measure maple syrup
Champagne, to top up
lemon rind strip, to decorate

Put the crushed ice into a
cocktail shaker. Pour the
Southern Comfort, lemon juice
and maple syrup over the ice
and shake until a frost forms.
Strain into a Champagne flute
and top up with Champagne.
Decorate with a lemon rind strip.

Champagne Cooler

crushed ice
1 measure brandy
1 measure Cointreau
Champagne, to top up
mint sprigs, to decorate

Put some crushed ice into a
Champagne glass. Pour the
brandy and Cointreau over
the ice. Top up with Champagne
and stir. Decorate with mint
sprigs.

Did you know?
Madame de Pompadour, mistress of
Louis XV, was described as being
'full of beauty after drinking it' when
she had been quaffing champagne.

Paddy's Night

3 ice cubes, cracked
1 measure green crème
   de menthe
1 measure Irish whiskey
Champagne, to top up

Put the cracked ice with the
crème de menthe and whiskey
into a cocktail shaker and
shake well. Strain into a
large wine glass and top up
with Champagne.

Paddy's Night ▶

Aria Classic

1 brown sugar cube
3 dashes Angostura bitters
1 measure Grand Marnier
Champagne, to top up
orange rind twist, to
    decorate

Drop the sugar cube into a
chilled Champagne flute and
shake the Angostura bitters
over it. Add the Grand Marnier
and stir briefly. Top up with
Champagne and decorate
with an orange rind twist.

Frobisher

chopped ice
2 dashes Angostura bitters
3 tablespoons gin
chilled Champagne, to
    top up
lemon peel twist, to
    decorate

Fill a highball glass with
chopped ice. Shake the bitters
over the ice. Pour in the gin
and top up with the chilled
Champagne. Squeeze the
lemon rind twist over the
drink and drop it in.

Champagne Julep

2 mint sprigs
1 tablespoon sugar syrup
crushed ice
1 measure brandy
Champagne, to top up

Muddle the mint with the sugar
syrup in a large wine glass. Fill
the glass with crushed ice, then
add the brandy. Top up with
Champagne and stir gently.

Pernod Fizz

1 measure Pernod
6 measures chilled
    Champagne
lime slice, to decorate

Put the Pernod into a
Champagne flute and swirl it
round to coat the inside of the
glass. Slowly pour in the chilled
Champagne, allowing the drink
to become cloudy. Decorate
with a lime slice.

Martini Royale

2½ measures ice-cold
    vodka
¼ measure crème de cassis
Champagne, to top up
lemon rind twist, to
    decorate

Pour the vodka into a chilled
Martini glass, then stir in the
cassis. Top up with Champagne,
then add a lemon rind twist.

Black Velvet

4 measures Guinness
4 measures Champagne

Pour the Guinness into a large
glass and carefully add the
Champagne.

Parisian Spring Punch

ice cubes, plus crushed ice,
    to serve
1½ measures Calvados
½ measure fresh lemon
    juice
½ measure Noilly Prat
1 teaspoon caster sugar
chilled Champagne, to
    top up
apple slices, to decorate

Put some ice cubes with the
Calvados, lemon juice, vermouth
and sugar into a shaker and
shake to mix. Strain over
crushed ice in a sling glass and
top up with chilled Champagne.
Decorate with apple slices.

Did you know?
Parisian Spring is an all-French
twist using Calvados, an apple-
flavoured liqueur from Normandy,
and Noilly Prat vermouth.

Russian Spring Punch

ice cubes
½ measure crème de cassis
1 measure fresh lemon juice
2 tablespoons sugar syrup
chilled Champagne, to
    top up
2 measures Absolut vodka
lemon slice and berries,
    to decorate

Fill a sling glass with ice cubes.
Pour over the crème de cassis,
lemon juice and sugar syrup.
Add the Champagne and vodka
at the same time (this prevents
excessive fizzing) and stir.
Decorate with a lemon slice
and berries.

Bombay Punch

ice cubes
1.2 litres (2 pints) brandy
1.2 litres (2 pints) sherry
150 ml (¼ pint) Maraschino
    liqueur
150 ml (¼ pint) orange
    Curaçao
5 litres (8 pints) chilled
    Champagne
2.5 litres (4 pints) sparkling
    mineral water
fruit in season and mint
    sprigs, to decorate

Put plenty of ice cubes into a
large punch bowl with all the
other ingredients and stir
gently. Decorate with fruits
and mint sprigs. Keep the
punch bowl packed with ice.
Serves 25–30

Bombay Punch ▸

Cool Shower

ice cubes
rind of 1 orange
3 measures sparkling dry
    white wine
1 measure Campari
2 measures orange juice

Put some ice cubes with the
orange rind into a wine goblet.
Add the sparkling wine,
Campari and orange juice.

White Sangria

2 large glasses dry
    white wine
2 measures lemon vodka
2 measures peach schnapps
2 measures peach purée
apple, lime, lemon and
    peach slices
ice cubes
1 measure lemon juice
1 measure lime juice
lemonade, to top up

Twelve hours before serving, put
the wine, vodka, schnapps and
peach purée in a jug with the
fruit slices and chill. Just before
serving, add some ice cubes and
the fruit juices and top up with
lemonade. Serve into glasses.
Serves 6

Loving Cup

8 sugar cubes
2 lemons
½ bottle medium or
    sweet sherry
¼ bottle brandy
1 bottle dry sparkling
    white wine

Rub the sugar cubes over the
lemons to absorb the zest.
Thinly peel the lemons and
remove as much of the pith
as possible. Thinly slice the
lemons and set aside. Put the
lemon rind, sherry, brandy and
sugar cubes into a jug and stir
until the sugar has dissolved.
Cover and chill for about 30
minutes. To serve, add the wine
to the jug and float the lemon
slices on top.
Serves 12

Glühwein

6 measures claret
3 sugar cubes
1 cinnamon stick
1 whole clove

Put all the ingredients into a small saucepan and bring to the boil. Serve in a large mug, steaming hot. Cider can be used instead of claret; add a dash of rum or apple brandy.

Chablis Cup

3 ripe peaches, skinned, stoned and sliced
1 orange, thinly sliced
cocktail cherries
3 teaspoons caster sugar
1 bottle chablis
4 measures Grand Marnier
4 measures Kirsch

Put the fruit and sugar in a punch bowl. Pour in the chablis, Grand Marnier and kirsch and stir. Cover and chill for 1 hour.
Serves 15–20

Glögg

2 bottles dry red wine, or
    1 bottle red wine and
    1 bottle port or Madeira
rind of 1 orange
20 cardamom pods,
    lightly crushed
2 cinnamon sticks
20 whole cloves
175 g (6 oz) blanched
    almonds
225 g (8 oz) raisins
225–350 g (8–12 oz) sugar
    cubes
300 ml (½ pint) Aquavit
    or brandy

Put the wine or wine and port or Madeira into a saucepan. Tie the orange and spices in a piece of muslin and add to pan. Add the almonds and raisins. Cook just below boiling point for 25 minutes, stirring occasionally.

Put a wire rack over the pan and put the sugar cubes on it. Warm the Aquavit or brandy and pour it over the sugar cubes to saturate them evenly. Set them alight: they will melt through the wire rack into the wine. Stir the glögg, then remove the spice bag. Serve hot, adding a few raisins and almonds to each cup.
Serves 15–20

Other Spirits and Liqueurs

From Caribbean Curaçao and Brazilian Cachaça to Italian grappa and Japanese sake, there is a whole array of liqueurs and spirits out there from every part of the globe. You can also be certain that for every drink, a cocktail has been created to include it. Baileys (cream), Kahlúa (coffee), Amaretto (almonds) and crème de cacao (chocolate) are some of the more popular ingredients used in modern cocktails, but the range of flavoured liqueurs is staggering – everything from banana to mint – and you'd need a bar the size of a hotel lobby to fit in the drinks required for every cocktail. It's a good idea to pick out the flavours and types of drinks that you really enjoy and start off with those. As long as you choose good-quality brands, you can't go too far wrong.

Classic Pimm's

2 measures Pimm's No 1
6–8 ice cubes
orange, lemon and
    cucumber slices
4 measures lemonade
mint or borage sprigs,
    to decorate

Pour the Pimm's into a highball
glass, add the ice cubes and the
fruit and cucumber slices, then
pour in the lemonade. Decorate
with mint or borage sprigs.

Did you know?
A combination of gin, bitters,
quinine and herbs, Pimm's No 1 was
created by London oyster bar
proprietor James Pimm in the
1840s. No English summer is
complete without it.

On the Lawn

ice cubes
1 measure Pimm's No 1
1 measure gin
2 measures lemonade
2 measures dry ginger ale
cucumber strips,
    blueberries and orange
    slices, to decorate

Fill a highball glass with ice
cubes, then add the Pimm's, gin,
lemonade and dry ginger ale.
Decorate with cucumber strips,
blueberries and orange slices.

Batida

crushed ice
2 measures cachaça
½ measure sugar syrup
½ measure fresh lemon
    juice
3 measures fruit juice
    (strawberry, pineapple
    or mango)

Fill a highball glass with
crushed ice. Pour the cachaça,
sugar syrup, lemon juice and
fruit juice into the glass and stir
to mix thoroughly.

Did you know?
A Brazilian classic using cachaça,
Batida is a traditional working
man's drink that has not transferred
as quickly from its native Brazil as
the Caipirinha (see page 219).

Cardamom and Raspberry Batida

4 raspberries
1 measure raspberry purée
2 measures cachaça
½ measure sugar syrup
½ measure lemon juice
seeds from 4 cardamom
    pods
ice cubes, plus crushed ice,
    to serve
lemon slices, to decorate

Muddle the raspberries and raspberry purée in a mixing glass. Add the cachaça, sugar syrup, lemon juice, cardamom seeds and ice cubes and stir well. Strain into a highball glass over crushed ice and decorate with lemon slices.

Batida Maracuja

ice cubes, plus crushed ice,
    to serve
2 measures cachaça
pulp of 2 passion fruit
1 measure sugar syrup
1 measure lemon juice
lemon slices, to decorate

Put some ice cubes with the cachaça, passion fruit pulp, syrup and lemon juice into a cocktail shaker and shake. Strain into a highball glass filled with crushed ice. Decorate with lemon slices.

Fuzzy Navel

1½ measures peach
    schnapps
6 measures orange juice

Pour the schnapps and orange juice into a large glass and stir well.

Strawberry and Hazelnut Lassi

crushed ice
3 strawberries, hulled
⅓ banana
1 measure Frangelico
1 measure Baileys Irish
  Cream
2 measures natural yogurt
3 mint leaves, plus 1 sprig
  to decorate

Put a scoop of crushed ice with
all the other ingredients into a
blender and blend until smooth.
Pour into a tall sling glass and
decorate with a mint sprig.

Toblerone

crushed ice
1 teaspoon clear honey
1 measure Frangelico
  hazelnut liqueur
1 measure Baileys Irish
  Cream
1 measure single cream
1 measure dark crème
  de cacao
chocolate shavings,
  to decorate

Put some crushed ice with the
honey, Frangelico, Baileys,
cream and crème de cacao into
a blender or food processor and
blend until slushy. Pour into a
hurricane glass and decorate
with chocolate shavings.

X-rated Milkshake

crushed ice
1 measure Frangelico
  hazelnut liqueur
1 measure Baileys Irish
  Cream
1 measure single cream
1 measure dark crème
  de cacao
½ measure clear honey
4 strawberries, hulled
⅓ banana
1 measure chocolate sauce,
  to decorate

Put some crushed ice with the
Frangelico, Baileys, cream, crème
de cacao, honey, strawberries and
banana into a blender or food
processor and blend until slushy.
Decorate the inside of a large
hurricane glass with chocolate
sauce and pour in the drink.

Caipirinha

1 lime, quartered
2 teaspoons cane sugar
crushed ice
2 measures cachaça

Muddle the lime quarters and sugar in an old-fashioned glass. Fill it with crushed ice and pour over the cachaça. Stir and add more ice as desired.

Kiwi Caipiroska

½ kiwi fruit, peeled
½ lime, cut into wedges
2 teaspoons sugar syrup
crushed ice
2 measures vodka
2 teaspoons kiwi fruit
 schnapps
kiwi fruit slice, to decorate

Muddle the kiwi fruit, lime and sugar syrup in an old-fashioned glass. Fill the glass with crushed ice, then add the vodka and stir. Add more ice, then drizzle the schnapps over the surface and decorate with a kiwi fruit slice.

Did you know?
A Caipirinha can only be made with cachaça – if it is made with vodka it is called a Caipiroska. Without a fruit flavour it can be a fairly bland drink, but with the addition of kiwi this twist is delicious.

Pansy

ice cubes
½ measure Pernod
several dashes grenadine
few dashes Angostura
 bitters
lemon rind twist, to
 decorate

Put some ice cubes into a cocktail shaker and pour over the Pernod, grenadine and bitters. Shake well. Pour into a chilled cocktail glass and decorate with a lemon twist.

Original Pisco Sour

ice cubes
2 measures Pisco
1 measure lemon juice
2 teaspoons caster sugar
1 egg white
3 dashes Angostura bitters

Put some ice cubes with the
Pisco, lemon juice, sugar and
egg white into a cocktail shaker
and shake well. Strain into an
old-fashioned glass. Add the
bitters to the drink's frothy head.

Velvet Hammer

ice cubes
1 measure Cointreau
1 measure Tia Maria
1 measure cream

Fill a cocktail shaker three-
quarters full with ice cubes.
Add all the other ingredients
and shake well. Strain into
a chilled cocktail glass.

Atacama Pisco Sour

crushed ice
1½ measures Pisco
½ measure blended
    Scotch whisky
1 measure lemon juice
1 measure sugar syrup
grated lemon rind, to
    decorate

Put a small scoop of crushed
ice with the Pisco, whisky,
lemon juice and sugar syrup
into a blender and blend until
smooth. Pour into a coupette
glass and decorate with
grated lemon rind.

Deaf Knees

½ measure chocolate
   schnapps
½ measure crème de
   menthe
½ measure Grand Marnier

Using the back of a bar spoon,
slowly float the crème de
menthe over the schnapps.
Pour the Grand Marnier over
the crème de menthe, in the
same way.

Did you know?
The layers of chocolate, mint and
orange deliver a powerful kick and
an explosion of flavours as you
knock back this shot.

Sake-tini

ice cubes
2½ measures sake
1 measure vodka
½ measure orange Curaçao
2 thin cucumber wheels,
   to decorate

Put the ice cubes into a mixing
glass, add the sake, vodka and
Curaçao and stir well. Strain
into a chilled cocktail glass and
add two cucumber wheels,
made by peeling the cucumber
in strips, lengthwise and then
thinly slicing.

Go West

ice cubes
½ measure Frangelico
1 measure Limoncello
1 measure dry white wine
½ measure sugar syrup
½ measure lemon juice
lemon rind twist, to
   decorate

Put some ice cubes with the
Frangelico, Limoncello, wine,
sugar syrup and juice into a
cocktail shaker and shake well.
Double strain into a chilled
Martini glass. Decorate with
a lemon rind twist.

Cucumber Sake-tini

ice cubes
2½ measures cucumber-
    infused sake
1½ measures gin
½ measure orange Curaçao
peeled cucumber slices,
    to decorate

Put some ice cubes with all the
other ingredients together in
a mixing glass and stir until
thoroughly chilled. Strain into a
chilled Martini glass. Decorate
with peeled cucumber slices.

Grasshopper

1 measure crème de cacao
1 measure crème de menthe
mint sprig, to decorate

Pour the crème de cacao into
a cocktail glass. Using the back
of a bar spoon, float the crème
de menthe over the crème
de cacao. Serve decorated
with a mint sprig.

Flaming Lamborghini

1 measure Kahlúa
1 measure Sambuca
1 measure Baileys Irish
    Cream
1 measure blue Curaçao

Pour the Kahlúa into a warmed
cocktail glass. Gently pour half
a measure of Sambuca over the
back of a spoon into the cocktail
glass, so that it floats on top.
Pour the Baileys and the blue
Curaçao into 2 short glasses.
Next, pour the remaining
Sambuca into a warmed wine
glass and carefully set it alight.
Pour it into the cocktail glass
with care. Pour the Baileys
and Curaçao into the lighted
cocktail glass at the same time.
Serve with a straw.

Grappa Strega

ice cubes
1 measure grappa
1 measure Strega
1 tablespoon lemon juice
1 tablespoon orange juice

Put some ice cubes into a mixing glass. Pour the grappa, Strega and fruit juices over the ice and stir. Strain into a chilled Martini glass.

Grappa Manhattan

ice cubes
2 measures grappa
1 measure Martini Rosso
½ measure Maraschino
    liqueur
2 dashes Angostura bitters
olive, to decorate

Put some ice cubes into a mixing glass. Pour the grappa, Martini, Maraschino and bitters over the ice and stir. Strain into a chilled Martini glass and decorate with an olive.

Banshee

ice cubes
1 measure white crème
    de cacao
1 measure crème de banane
1 measure single cream

Put some ice cubes into a cocktail shaker. Pour the crème de cacao, crème de banane and cream over the ice. Shake vigorously. Strain and serve straight up.

Money Shot

1 measure well-chilled
   Jagermeister
1 measure well-chilled
   Rumple Minze
   (peppermint liqueur)

Pour the Jagermeister into a
shot glass. Using the back of
a bar spoon, slowly float the
Rumple Minze over the
Jagermeister.

Fireball

½ measure ice-cold
   kümmel
½ measure Goldschlager
½ measure absinthe

Pour the kümmel into a shot
glass. Using the back of a bar
spoon, slowly float the
Goldschlager over the kümmel.
Pour the absinthe over the
Goldschlager in the same way.

Slippery Nipple

1 measure Sambuca
½ measure Baileys
   Irish Cream

Pour the Sambuca into a shot
glass. Using the back of a bar
spoon, slowly float the Baileys
over the Sambuca.

Did you know?
Slippery Nipple is popular in bars
everywhere. It is easy to drink, but
has a hidden kick, so be prepared to
make more than one round of these.

Papa G

ice cubes
1 measure Amaretto
   di Saronno
1 dash lemon juice
1 dash sugar syrup
1 drop Angostura bitters

Put some ice cubes with all the ingredients into a cocktail shaker and shake briefly. Strain into a shot glass.

B-4-12

½ measure Amaretto
   di Saronno
½ measure Baileys Irish
   Cream
½ measure chilled Absolut
   Kurant vodka

Pour the Amaretto into a shot glass. Using the back of a bar spoon, slowly float the Baileys over the Amaretto. Pour the Absolut Kurant over the Baileys in the same way.

Did you know?
Layered cocktails like this will keep for at least an hour in the refrigerator, so you can make several in advance.

B-52

½ measure Kahlúa
½ measure Baileys Irish
   Cream
½ measure Grand Marnier

Pour the Kahlúa into a shot glass. Using the back of a bar spoon, slowly float the Baileys over the Kahlúa. Pour the Grand Marnier over the Baileys in the same way.

Brain Haemorrhage

1 measure peach schnapps
1 dash Baileys Irish Cream
3 drops grenadine

Pour the schnapps into a chilled shot glass. Using the back of a bar spoon, slowly float the Baileys over the schnapps. Very gently, drop the grenadine on top of the Baileys – it will gradually ease through this top layer.

Cowgirl

1 measure chilled peach
    schnapps
½ measure Baileys Irish
    Cream
peach wedge, to decorate

Pour the chilled schnapps into a shot glass. Using the back of a bar spoon, slowly layer the Baileys over the schnapps. Place a peach wedge on the rim of the glass, to be eaten after the shot has been drunk.

Did you know?
The flavour of peach schnapps with Baileys is a winning combination, and the slice of ripe peach adds a touch of decadence to this shot.

383

1 teaspoon Frangelico
    hazelnut liqueur
1 measure chilled
    Stolichnaya Razberi
    vodka
orange wedge dusted with
    sugar, to decorate

Put the Frangelico into a shot glass, then add the vodka. Decorate with the sugared orange wedge. Drink the shot in one gulp, then eat the orange.

383 ▸

Moth & Moose

½ measure Passoa liqueur
½ measure Grey Goose
    l'Orange vodka

Pour the Passoa into a shot
glass. Using the back of a bar
spoon, slowly float the vodka
over the Passoa.

Strawberry Eclair

1 strawberry, hulled
1 lime wedge
½ measure Frangelico
    hazelnut liqueur
½ measure wild
    strawberry liqueur
ice cubes

Muddle the strawberry and the
lime wedge in a cocktail shaker.
Add the liqueurs and some ice
cubes, then shake briefly and
strain into a shot glass.

Did you know?
There is a real strawberry explosion
here, with liqueurs and fresh fruit
fighting for the attention of your
taste buds.

PCP

ice cubes
¾ measure Xante pear
    liqueur
1 dash strawberry liqueur
1 dash pear liqueur
1 dash lemon juice
1 dash vanilla syrup

Put some ice cubes into a
cocktail shaker with all the
other ingredients and shake
briefly. Strain into a chilled
shot glass.

Absinthe Minded

ice cubes
1 measure absinthe
1 dash fresh lemon juice
1 dash Chambord

Put some ice cubes with all the ingredients into a cocktail shaker and shake briefly. Strain into a chilled shot glass.

Bubble Gum

ice cubes
½ measure Pisang
   Ambon liqueur
½ measure Malibu
1 dash fraise liqueur
1 dash pineapple juice

Put some ice cubes with all the ingredients into a cocktail shaker and shake briefly. Strain into a shot glass.

QF

½ measure Kahlúa
dash Midori liqueur
½ measure Baileys
   Irish Cream

Pour the Kahlúa into a shot glass. Using the back of a bar spoon, slowly float the Midori over the Kahlúa. Pour the Baileys over the Midori in the same way.

Alcohol-free

These days many people have dropped alcohol from their diet for a number of reasons: anyone following a weight-loss diet may take alcohol out of the equation, while those conscious of their health or pregnant may have eliminated alcoholic beverages for those reasons. Anyone who has a problem with alcohol and is trying to beat that addiction will want to avoid alcohol at all costs. And there are people who abstain for religious reasons as well. Another major factor is the drink-driving laws; if you are the designated driver, you certainly won't be drinking anything alcoholic. But no one wants to be left out when you are making dazzling drink combinations. There are dozens of delicious and exciting non-alcoholic cocktails, based on exotic fruits, herbs and spices, bitters and sodas, to add to your cocktail repertoire and to suit every palate.

Cool Passion

500 ml (17 fl oz) orange
    and passion fruit juice
1 litre (1¾ pints)
    pineapple juice
1.5 litres (2½ pints)
    lemonade
crushed ice
blackberries and mint
    sprigs, to decorate

Pour the juices into a large jug.
Stir well to mix. Just before
serving, stir in the lemonade.
Pour into glasses filled with
crushed ice and decorate with
a blackberry and a mint sprig.
Serves 20

Lemonade on the Rocks

½ lemon, roughly chopped
3 teaspoons icing sugar
150 ml (¼ pint) water
ice cubes
soda water or mineral
    water, to top up
lemon or lime slices,
    to decorate

Put the lemon, 2 teaspoons
of the icing sugar and half the
water into a blender or food
processor and blend for a few
seconds. Add the remaining
water and blend again. Taste
and add more icing sugar if
required, then blend again.
Strain into a tumbler and
top up with soda or mineral
water. Decorate with lemon or
lime slices.

Bitter Sweet

crushed ice
150 ml (¼ pint) sparkling
    mineral water
2 dashes Angostura bitters
6–8 mint leaves
lemon or lime slices,
    to decorate

Put the crushed ice into a
cocktail shaker, pour over
2 tablespoons of the mineral
water and the bitters and add
the mint leaves. Shake until a
frost forms. Pour into a chilled
glass, top up with the remaining
mineral water and decorate
with lemon or lime slices.

Limeade

6 limes
125 g (4 oz) caster sugar
750 ml (1¼ pints)
   boiling water
pinch of salt
ice cubes
lime wedges and mint
   leaves, to decorate

Halve the limes, then squeeze
the juice into a large jug. Put
the squeezed lime halves into a
heatproof jug with the sugar
and boiling water and leave to
infuse for 15 minutes. Add the
salt, stir the infusion well, then
strain it into the jug with the
lime juice. Add 6 ice cubes,
cover and chill for 2 hours or
until chilled. To serve, put
3–4 ice cubes in each glass and
pour the limeade over them.
Add a lime wedge and a mint
leaf to decorate.
Serves 8

Midsummer Punch

125 g (4 oz) sugar
300 ml (½ pint) water
300 ml (½ pint) orange juice
300 ml (½ pint) pineapple
   juice
600 ml (1 pint) cold weak
   tea, strained
orange, lemon, apple and
   pineapple slices
crushed ice
300 ml (½ pint) dry
   ginger ale
mint sprigs, to decorate

Put the sugar and water into a
saucepan and stir over a low
heat until the sugar has
dissolved. Leave to cool, then
pour into a large jug or bowl.
Stir in the fruit juices and cold
tea, then add the fruit slices and
some crushed ice. To serve,
pour into tall glasses and top up
with the dry ginger ale.
Decorate with mint sprigs.
Serves 8–10

Alcohol-free Sangria

1 litre (1¾ pints)
   orange juice
sugar syrup, to taste
2 litres (3½ pints) red
   grape juice
juice of 6 lemons
juice of 6 limes
20–30 ice cubes
orange, lemon and lime
   slices, to decorate

Pour the orange juice and sugar
syrup to taste, into a punch
bowl and stir. Add the fruit
juices and stir well to mix. Add
the ice cubes, then float the
fruit slices on top.
Serves 20

Grapefruit Cooler

125 g (4 oz) sugar
4 measures water
handful of mint sprigs
juice of 4 large lemons
450 ml (¾ pint) grapefruit
  juice
crushed ice
soda water, to top up
mint sprigs, to decorate

Put the sugar and water into a heavy-based saucepan and stir over a low heat until the sugar has dissolved. Leave to cool. Crush the mint leaves and stir into the syrup. Cover and leave to stand for about 12 hours, then strain into a jug. Add the fruit juices to the strained syrup and stir well. Fill 6 old-fashioned glasses or tumblers with crushed ice and pour the cooler into the glasses. Top up with soda water and decorate with mint sprigs.
Serves 6

Warbine Cooler

2 dashes Angostura bitters
1 dash lime juice
ginger beer, to top up
lime slices, to decorate

Stir the bitters and lime juice together in a large wine glass. Top up with ginger beer and decorate with lime slices. Serve with a straw.

Clayton's Pussyfoot

3 ice cubes, cracked
½ measure lemon syrup
½ measure orange juice
1 measure cola

Put all the ingredients into a cocktail shaker and shake well. Strain into a cocktail glass.

Iced Mint Tea

12 mint sprigs
1 lemon, finely chopped
1 tablespoon sugar
1.2 litres (2 pints) weak
    tea, strained
ice cubes
lemon slices, to decorate

Chop up the mint sprigs and put them into a large heatproof jug with the lemon and sugar. Pour the tea into the jug and leave to infuse for 20–30 minutes. Strain into another jug and chill until required. To serve, pour into tumblers or tall glasses filled with ice cubes and decorate each glass with lemon slices.
Serves 4

Cranberry Crush

crushed ice
1.8 litres (3 pints) cranberry
    juice
600 ml (1 pint) orange juice
600 ml (1 pint) dry ginger
    ale
orange and lemon wedges,
    to decorate

Half-fill a large punch bowl with crushed ice. Pour in the fruit juices and stir to mix. Top up with the dry ginger ale and decorate with orange and lemon wedges.
Serves 15

Did you know?
For a special occasion, float red rose petals on top of the punch.

Fruit Punch

600 ml (1 pint) orange juice
600 ml (1 pint) apple juice
150 ml (¼ pint) water
½ teaspoon ground ginger
½ teaspoon mixed spice
soft brown sugar (optional)
1 apple, thinly sliced,
    to decorate

Put the fruit juices, water and spices into a saucepan and bring gently to the boil, adding sugar to taste, if required. Simmer the mixture for 5 minutes. Pour the punch into a warmed bowl and float the apple slices on top.
Serves 6

Tropical Treat

900 ml (1½ pints) natural
  yogurt
1 large ripe pineapple,
  peeled and roughly
  chopped
300 ml (½ pint) sparkling
  mineral water
ice cubes
sugar syrup, to taste
mint sprigs, to decorate

Put the yogurt, pineapple
and mineral water into a
food processor and blend until
smooth, in batches if necessary.
Put the ice cubes into a tall jug,
then pour in the drink through
a very fine strainer. Stir, then
add sugar syrup to taste and stir
again. Pour into tall glasses and
decorate with mint sprigs.
Serves 4

Nursery Fizz

crushed ice
3 measures orange juice
3 measures dry ginger ale
cocktail cherry and orange
  slice, to decorate

Fill a large wine glass with
crushed ice and pour in the
orange juice and ginger ale.
Decorate with a cherry and an
orange slice impaled on a
cocktail stick.

Prohibition
Punch

4 measures sugar syrup
12 measures lemon juice
900 ml (1½ pints) apple
  juice
ice cubes
2.5 litres (4 pints) dry
  ginger ale
orange slices, to decorate

Put the sugar syrup and fruit
juices into a large chilled jug
and stir. Add the ice cubes and
pour in the dry ginger ale.
Decorate with orange slices.
Serves 25–30

Green Devil

juice of 1½ limes, strained
1 teaspoon Angostura
    bitters
3 ice cubes
sparkling mineral water,
    to top up

Put the lime juice and bitters
into a mixing glass and stir
together. Put the ice cubes into a
tall glass, then pour in the drink.
Top up with mineral water.

Spiced Ginger Punch

2 oranges
cloves, to taste
1 cm (½ inch) piece of fresh
    root ginger, peeled and
    grated
2 litres (3½ pints) dry
    ginger ale
cinnamon stick

Stud the oranges with the
cloves, then bake them in a
preheated oven at 180°C
(350°F), Gas Mark 4 for about
25 minutes, until they are a
rich, golden colour. Cut the
oranges into slices using a
sharp knife, then put them into
a saucepan with the grated
ginger, dry ginger ale and the
cinnamon stick. Bring steadily
to boiling point, but do not boil.
Remove the cinnamon stick,
then pour the punch into
heatproof glasses and serve.
Serves 12

Tenderberry

crushed ice
6–8 strawberries, hulled
1 measure grenadine
1 measure double cream
1 measure dry ginger ale
ground ginger
strawberry, to decorate

Put some crushed ice with the
strawberries, grenadine and
cream into a blender or food
processor and blend for
30 seconds. Pour into a glass.
Add the dry ginger ale and
stir. Sprinkle a little ground
ginger on top and decorate
with a strawberry.

Carrot Cream

5 ice cubes
2 measures carrot juice
3 measures single cream
1 egg yolk
1 measure orange juice
orange slices, to decorate

Put the ice cubes in a tall glass.
Put the carrot juice, cream, egg
yolk and orange juice into a
cocktail shaker and shake well.
Pour the carrot drink over the
ice. Decorate with orange slices
and serve immediately.

Brown Horny Toad

4–5 crushed ice cubes
2 measures pineapple juice
2 measures orange juice
1 measure lemon juice
1 tablespoon grenadine
1 teaspoon sugar syrup
pinch of ground cinnamon
pinch of ground cloves
orange and lemon slices,
    to decorate

Put the ice cubes into a cocktail
shaker. Pour in the fruit juices,
and add the grenadine then add
the sugar syrup and spices.
Shake until a frost forms. Strain
into a highball glass and
decorate with orange and
lemon slices.

Did you know?
To make a Green Horny Toad,
substitute lime juice for the orange
juice and use lime syrup instead of
the grenadine.

Caribbean Cocktail

1 mango, peeled and stoned
1 banana
juice of 1 orange
1 dash lime juice
4–5 ice cubes
lime slices, to decorate

Put the mango, banana and
fruit juices in a blender or food
processor and blend until
smooth. Pour the cocktail over
the ice cubes in a large highball
glass. Decorate with lime slices.

River Cruise

500 g (1 lb) cantaloupe
    melon pulp
grated rind and juice of
    2 lemons
2 tablespoons sugar
600 ml (1 pint) chilled
    soda water

Remove and discard any melon
seeds. Put the pulp into a
blender or food processor and
blend until smooth. Scrape the
purée into a large jug. Put the
lemon rind and juice into a
small saucepan with the sugar
and stir over a low heat until
the sugar has dissolved. Strain
the lemon mixture into the
melon purée, mix well and chill.
Stir in the chilled soda water
just before serving.
Serves 4–6

Did you know?
**If you have a juicer, put the melon
flesh through it to make a delicious
clear juice to use in this drink.**

San Francisco

3 ice cubes
1 measure orange juice
1 measure lemon juice
1 measure pineapple juice
1 measure grapefruit juice
2 dashes grenadine
1 egg white
soda water, to top up
lemon and lime slices,
    to decorate
cocktail cherry and orange
    rind spiral, to decorate

Put the ice cubes into a cocktail
shaker and pour in the fruit
juices, grenadine and egg white.
Shake well, then strain into a
large goblet. Top up with soda
water and decorate with lemon
and lime slices and a cocktail
cherry impaled on a cocktail
stick, and an orange rind spiral.
Serve with a straw.

Bugs Bunny

4–6 ice cubes
2 measures carrot juice
2 measures orange juice
1 dash Tabasco sauce
1 celery stick, to decorate

Put the ice into a tumbler. Pour
the carrot and orange juices
over the ice, add a dash of
Tabasco sauce and decorate
with a celery stick.

Anita

3 ice cubes
1 measure orange juice
1 measure lemon juice
3 dashes Angostura bitters
soda water, to top up
lemon and orange slices,
    to decorate

Put the ice cubes into a cocktail shaker. Pour in the fruit juices and bitters and shake well. Strain into a tumbler and top up with soda water. Decorate with lemon and orange slices.

Tomato and Cucumber Cooler

crushed ice
5 measures tomato juice
25 g (1 oz) cucumber, peeled
2 dashes lemon juice
2 dashes Worcestershire
    sauce
salt and pepper
cucumber slice, to decorate

Put a little crushed ice into a blender or food processor. Add the tomato juice, cucumber, lemon juice, Worcestershire sauce and salt and pepper to taste and blend until smooth. Pour the drink into a cocktail glass and decorate with a cucumber slice.

Romanov Fizz

1 ice cube
4–5 ripe strawberries,
    hulled
2 measures orange juice
2 measures soda water

Put the strawberries and orange juice into a blender or food processor and blend until smooth. Put the ice cube in a sour or wine glass and add the strawberry liquid. Pour the soda water into the blender or food processor, blend briefly and use to top up the glass. Stir briskly and serve.

Romanov Fizz ▶

Coco-oco

crushed ice
4 teaspoons creamed
    coconut or coconut syrup
2 teaspoons lemon juice
1 teaspoon Maraschino
    syrup
3½ measures full-fat milk
4 dashes Angostura bitters
pineapple leaf and wedge,
    to decorate
cocktail cherry, to decorate

Put the crushed ice into a
blender or food processor and
add the creamed coconut or
coconut syrup, lemon juice,
Maraschino syrup, milk and
bitters. Blend for a few seconds.
Pour into a tall glass and
decorate with a pineapple leaf
and wedge and a cherry.

Guavarama

crushed ice
7 measures guava juice
2 teaspoons lime juice
4 teaspoons blackcurrant
    syrup
5 dashes rum essence
melon slice, to decorate

Put some crushed ice into a
blender or food processor
and add the fruit juices,
blackcurrant syrup and rum
essence. Blend thoroughly,
then strain into a chilled
cocktail glass and decorate
with a melon slice.

Cranberry, Raspberry and Orange Crush

3½ measures cranberry
    juice
1¾ measures orange juice
250 ml (4 oz) raspberries
1½ scoops orange sorbet,
    plus extra to decorate
sugar syrup (optional)

Put the cranberry juice, orange
juice, raspberries and sorbet
into a blender or food processor
and blend until frothy. Taste
and add sugar syrup, if
required. Serve in a chilled
cocktail glass with an extra
scoop of sorbet.

Appleade

1 dessert apple
200 ml (7 fl oz) boiling water
pinch of sugar
ice cubes
apple slices, to decorate

Chop the apple and place in a
bowl. Pour the boiling water
over the apples and add the
sugar. Leave to stand for 10
minutes, then strain into a jug
and allow to cool. Pour over
some ice cubes in tall glasses
and decorate with apple slices.
Serve with straws.

Carib Cream

crushed ice
1 small banana, chopped
1 measure lemon juice
1 measure full-fat milk
1 teaspoon finely
   chopped walnuts

Put some crushed ice with the
banana, lemon juice and milk
into a blender or food processor
and blend at maximum speed
until smooth. Pour into a
cocktail glass and sprinkle the
chopped walnuts on top just
before serving.

Frosty Lime

1 scoop lime sorbet
1 measure grapefruit juice
4 teaspoons mint syrup
mint strips and lemon
   slices, to decorate

Put the sorbet, grapefruit juice
and syrup into a blender or food
processor and blend at high
speed for about 30 seconds.
Strain into a Champagne glass
and decorate with mint strips
and lemon slices.

Parson's Special

3 ice cubes
4 dashes grenadine
4 measures orange juice
1 egg yolk

Put the ice cubes into a cocktail
shaker and pour over the
grenadine, orange juice and
egg yolk. Shake well, then
strain into a tumbler.

Apple Eye

crushed ice
2 measures apple juice
½ measure blackcurrant
    syrup
1 measure double cream
ground cinnamon
apple slices, to decorate

Put some crushed ice with the
apple juice, blackcurrant syrup
and cream into a blender or
food processor and blend at
maximum speed for 30 seconds.
Pour into a cocktail glass and
sprinkle a little ground
cinnamon on top. Decorate
with apple slices.

Peach, Pear and Raspberry Crush

crushed ice
1 ripe peach, skinned,
    stoned and chopped
1 ripe pear, peeled, cored
    and chopped
125 g (4 oz) raspberries
7 measures peach juice
pear slices, to decorate

Put some crushed ice with the
peach, pear, raspberries and
peach juice into a blender or
food processor and blend until
smooth. Serve in cocktail
glasses and decorate with
pear slices.
Serves 2–3

Café Astoria

3 ice cubes, crushed
1½ measures coffee
   essence
2 measures full-fat milk
1 measure pineapple juice
½ measure lemon juice
chocolate shavings, to
   decorate

Put the crushed ice with the
coffee essence, milk, pineapple
juice and lemon juice into a
blender or food processor and
blend at maximum speed for
30 seconds. Pour into a cocktail
glass and sprinkle the chocolate
shavings on top just before
serving.

Egg Nog

cracked ice
1 egg
sugar syrup, to taste
8 measures full-fat milk
grated nutmeg, to decorate

Put some cracked ice with the
egg, sugar syrup and milk into a
cocktail shaker and shake well.
Strain into a large goblet and
sprinkle with grated nutmeg.

Tutti Frutti Verbena Cocktail

3 sachets verbena tea
600 ml (1 pint) boiling water
juice of 2 oranges
juice of 2 lemons
150 ml (¼ pint) apricot juice
150 ml (¼ pint) pineapple
   juice
ice cubes

Put the sachets of verbena tea
into a heatproof jug, pour over
the boiling water and leave to
infuse. When the tea is cold,
remove the sachets from the jug.
Pour the tea into another jug
and add the fruit juices and a
few ice cubes.
Serves 4–6

Did you know?
Try different flavours of fruit tea,
such as elderflower, rosehip or
cranberry in place of the verbena
tea in this refreshing cocktail.

Florentine Coffee

hot espresso coffee
1 drop almond essence
1 sugar cube (optional)

Pour the coffee into a warmed cup or heatproof glass. Add the almond essence and sugar, if using, and stir.

Iced Apple Tea

450 ml (¾ pint) chilled
    weak tea
450 ml (¾ pint) apple juice
juice of 1 lemon
1 teaspoon sugar (optional)
ice cubes
lemon and orange slices,
    to decorate
mint sprigs, to decorate

Mix the tea with the apple juice, lemon juice and sugar, if using. Add plenty of ice cubes and decorate with the lemon and orange slices and mint sprigs. Serve in tumblers or tea glasses. Serves 6–8

Catherine Blossom

7 measures orange juice
2 teaspoons maple syrup
2 scoops orange sorbet
soda water, to top up

Put the orange juice, maple syrup and orange sorbet into a blender or food processor and blend for 15 seconds. Pour into a tall glass and top up with soda water.

Did you know?

Good-quality maple syrup makes a wonderful flavouring for drinks, with its complex winey taste. But if you can't find it, use clear honey instead – try orange blossom honey for extra interest.

Limey

3 ice cubes, cracked
1 measure lime juice
½ measure lemon juice
½ egg white
cocktail cherry, to decorate

Put the cracked ice with the
fruit juices and egg white into a
cocktail shaker and shake well.
Strain into a cocktail glass and
decorate with a cherry.

Virgin Colada

crushed ice
1 measure coconut cream
2 measures pineapple juice
pineapple wedge, to
    decorate

Put some crushed ice with the
coconut cream and pineapple
juice into a blender or food
processor and blend, or shake
in a cocktail shaker. Pour into
a tall glass and decorate with
a pineapple wedge.

St Clements

4 ice cubes
2 measures orange juice
2 measures bitter lemon
orange slice, to decorate

Put the ice cubes into a
tumbler. Pour the orange juice
and bitter lemon over the ice,
stir together and decorate with
an orange slice.

Jersey Lily

ice cubes
5 measures sparkling
   apple juice
2 dashes Angostura bitters
¼ teaspoon caster sugar
cocktail cherry, to decorate

Put some ice cubes with the
apple juice, bitters and sugar in
a cocktail shaker. Shake well,
then strain into a wine glass.
Decorate with a cherry.

Did you know?
Sparkling grape juice, either red or
white, makes a refreshing substitute
for the apple juice.

Grenadine Soda

½ scoop orange sorbet
½ scoop raspberry sorbet
1½ tablespoons grenadine
juice of ½ lime
1 scoop vanilla ice cream
4 measures soda water
finely chopped orange
   slice and raspberries,
   to decorate

Put the sorbets, grenadine and
lime juice into a blender or food
processor and blend until
slushy. Pour into a glass and put
the vanilla ice cream on top.
Top up with soda water. Stir
gently and decorate with the
finely chopped orange slice and
raspberries. Serve with straws.

Pink Tonic

4–6 ice cubes
2–3 dashes Angostura
   bitters
8 measures tonic water
lime wedge, to decorate

Put the ice cubes into a
tumbler. Shake the bitters over
the ice, add the tonic water
and stir well. Decorate with
a lime wedge.

Shirley Temple

4–5 ice cubes
1 dash grenadine
dry ginger ale
2 cocktail cherries,
    to decorate

Put the ice cubes into a glass.
Add the grenadine and top up
with dry ginger ale. Decorate
with 2 cherries impaled on a
cocktail stick.

Honeymoon

crushed ice
1 measure maple syrup or
    clear honey
4 teaspoons lime juice
1 measure orange juice
1 measure apple juice
cocktail cherry, to decorate

Put some crushed ice into a
cocktail shaker and add the
maple syrup or honey, and fruit
juices. Shake well, then strain
into a chilled cocktail glass.
Decorate with a cherry impaled
on a cocktail stick.

Keep Sober

ice cubes
½ measure grenadine
½ measure lemon syrup
3 measures tonic water
soda water, to top up

Put some ice cubes with the
grenadine, lemon syrup and
tonic water into a tumbler
and stir together. Top up with
soda water.

Did you know?
For a tangier version of Keep Sober,
replace the grenadine with lime
syrup and decorate the drink with
lime slices.

Glossary

Blend It is sometimes necessary to blend a cocktail which uses fresh fruit or crushed ice. This can be done by simply adding your ingredients to an electric blender or liquidizer, usually along with crushed or cracked ice, and blending for about 10 seconds. Carbonated liquids should never be added to a blender as it is likely to cause the mixture to explode.

Build Simply fill your glass with ice, pour in the ingredients and serve.

Dash Ingredients with a very strong flavour, such as syrups and bitters, are usually added in very small quantities. A dash is literally a very small amount splashed into a drink.

Float This refers to a liquid or cream which forms a separate layer on top of another liquid. To do this, gently pour the liquid over the back of a spoon, making sure the spoon is touching the inside of the glass and is in contact with the drink.

Frappé A cocktail poured over finely crushed ice and often served with a long straw so that the drink and the ice can be sipped together from the bottom of the glass.

Frosting A frosted glass has a coated rim, usually of sugar or salt. To get this effect, wet the rim of the glass with water or egg white then dip it in your chosen coating.

Muddle Fruit and herbs are often crushed in the bottom of a glass using a wooden pestle in order to release their juices and extract as much flavour as possible.

Neat A drink served without ice or a mixer.

On the rocks A drink served over a glassful of ice cubes. This serves to dilute the liquor slightly as well as chilling it.

Shake The technique is to put all the ingredients into a cocktail shaker along with cubed or cracked ice then to shake vigorously using both hands until the outside of the shaker is frosty. The ice acts as a beater in the shaker as well as chilling the drink.

Spiral A strip of rind cut from a citrus fruit in a long spiral. This can be added to a drink for extra flavour or simply as decoration.

Stir Used for clear drinks whose appearance would be spoiled by vigorous shaking. Place the ingredients in a mixing glass and stir gently with a long-handled spoon then strain into a fresh glass.

Straight up A drink served without ice, usually in a tall glass.

Strain After a drink has been shaken or stirred, it is often necessary to strain the liquid into a glass to remove the ice or any fragments of fruit. This is done using a strainer. Some cocktail shakers come with their own strainer that fits over the shaker or mixing glass. Certain cocktails require double straining using a second strainer over the glass. This ensures a clearer liquid.

Sugar syrup Used as a sweetening agent, sugar syrup is an essential ingredient in any well-equipped bar. It is a mix of three parts sugar to one part water and comes in a variety of flavours.

Swizzle stick This is a stirrer that is served with the drink. It acts as a decoration but can also be used to stir the drink when ingredients settle at the bottom of the glass.

Twist This is used as a decoration and to add extra flavour. It is made by cutting a long piece of peel, usually from a citrus fruit, and twisting it in the middle to release the oil from the outer rind.

Recommended Cocktails

The following drinks, divided into categories by their size or type of glass, are particularly popular. If you are new to mixing cocktails, you might like to try some of these to start with. Drinks marked ☆ are non-alcoholic.

Long Drinks

Short Drinks

Shots

Classic Cocktails

Wines and Champagnes

Index

Italic page references refer to illustrations.

Acknowledgements

Photography by © Octopus
Publishing Group Limited/
Stephen Conroy.

Other photography:

**Octopus Publishing Group
Limited**/Jean Cazals 15 top left, 110
bottom left, 246 bottom left; /Sandra
Lane 24 top centre, 212 bottom
right, 235 top centre; /William
Lingwood 19 top left; /Neil Mersh
15 top right, 15 bottom right, 16, 22
bottom right, 25 top centre, 29 top
left, 35 bottom centre, 36 bottom
centre, 40, 56 bottom centre, 66
bottom left, 85 bottom centre, 90
bottom left, 91 top centre, 108 top
right, 108 bottom left, 117 bottom
left, 133 top centre, 142 top left, 158
top centre, 234 bottom left, 236
bottom right, 238 bottom left, 239
bottom centre; /Peter Myers 82 top
right, 89 top centre, 118 top centre,
170 top centre, 176 bottom left, 194,
214, 236 top left; /Peter
Myers/NeilMersh 11 bottom, 22 top
centre, 100 bottom left, 174 bottom
left, 218 top right; /William Reavell
1, 5, 6, 12 right, 12 bottom centre, 13
top centre, 13 centre left, 13 bottom
right, 14 top right, 14 bottom left, 15
centre right, 20 bottom centre, 27
bottom left, 29 bottom right, 37 top
left, 43 bottom right, 44 top right, 47
bottom right, 48, 51 top centre, 51
bottom right, 52 top centre, 54
bottom centre, 57 top centre, 61 top
right, 62 top centre, 63 top right, 63
bottom left, 64 bottom left, 73
bottom left, 80, 86 bottom left, 98
bottom right, 100 bottom right, 101
top left, 103 top centre, 103 bottom
left, 114, 125 bottom left, 128 top
centre, 130 bottom right, 131 top
left, 132 top centre, 136 top centre,
136 bottom left, 137 bottom centre,
138 bottom right, 139 top right, 146,
148 bottom right, 148 bottom left,
149 top centre, 150 bottom centre,
151 bottom right, 152 bottom left,
153 top centre, 155, 156 bottom
centre, 157 bottom centre, 159 top
centre, 159 bottom left, 160 bottom
centre, 163 bottom left, 164 bottom
left, 165 top left, 165 bottom centre,
170 bottom left, 171 bottom centre,
173, 174 top right, 175 bottom left,
178 top right, 178 bottom left, 179
bottom centre, 181, 184 bottom
centre, 185 top centre, 185 bottom
left, 186 top right, 186 bottom
centre, 187 bottom centre, 188 top
right, 188 bottom left, 190 bottom
left, 191 bottom centre, 198 top
centre, 199 top centre, 200 top
centre, 200 bottom left, 203 bottom
centre, 204 top centre, 204 bottom
left, 205 bottom centre, 207, 208 top
right, 211, 212 top centre, 213 top
centre, 222 top centre, 230, 232
bottom left, 233 top left, 237 top
right, 241, 242 bottom left, 244
bottom right, 245 top centre, 247 top
centre, 248 bottom right, 249 top
left, 249 bottom centre; /Ian Wallace
243 bottom right.

Executive Editor: **Sarah Ford**
Project Editor: **Kate Tuckett**
Editorial Assistant: **Pauline Thomas**
Executive Art Editor: **Joanna
  MacGregor**
Designer: **Colin Goody**
Picture Researcher: **Sophie Delpech**
Production Controller: **Nigel Reed**